creative

ACTIVITIES FOR

Plot,
Character
& Setting

TERESA GRAINGER
KATHY GOOUCH &
ANDREW LAMBIRTH

**AGES
9–11**

Authors
Teresa Grainger,
Kathy Goouch and
Andrew Lambirth

Editor
Roanne Charles

Assistant Editor
Aileen Lalor

Series Designers
Anthony Long and
Joy Monkhouse

Designer
Erik Ivens

Illustrations
Garry Walton

Cover image
Joy Monkhouse

The publishers would like to thank:

Scholastic Children's Books Ltd for the use of an illustration 'Little Head Riding Pudd' from *Arabian Frights and Other Gories* by Michael Rosen, illustrated by Chris Fisher Illustration © 1994, Chris Fisher (1994, André Deutsch Children's Books).

DC Thomson and Co Ltd for the use of the front page of *The Dandy* © DC Thomson and Co Ltd. www.dandy.com.

The Watts Publishing Group for the use of images from *Clarice Bean, That's Me* by Lauren Child © 1999, Lauren Child (1999, Orchard Books).

The staff and pupils at **The Ferncumbe Primary School**.

The authors would like to thank: all the energetic and creative professionals on the Advanced Certificate in Creativity in Literacy Learning, and the Masters courses in Language and Literacy who have trialled these ideas in their classrooms.

Published by Scholastic Ltd,
Villiers House,
Clarendon Avenue,
Leamington Spa,
Warwickshire CV32 5PR

www.scholastic.co.uk

Text © 2004 Teresa Grainger, Kathy Goouch and Andrew Lambirth
© 2004 Scholastic Ltd

Designed using Adobe InDesign

Printed and bound by Tien Wah Press Ltd, Singapore

4 5 6 7 8 9   6 7 8 9 0 1 2 3

British Library Cataloguing-in-Publication Data

A catalogue record for this book is available from the British Library.

ISBN 0-439-97113-6

The rights of Teresa Grainger, Kathy Goouch and Andrew Lambirth to be identified as the Authors of this work have been asserted by them in accordance with the Copyright, Designs and Patents Act 1988.

Contents

Introduction

Enthusiasm for and engagement with stories play a critical role in children's development as readers, writers and tellers of tales. In school, educators need to continue to offer children opportunities to engage in powerful fiction, to enter imaginary worlds, to examine the construction of texts and to make use of and build on this knowledge in their writing. Between the ages of 9 and 11, children become more conscious of how narrative works and become conversant with the various elements of stories, including: plot, character, setting, theme and language. In the process of reading, enjoying and studying texts, these aspects of story grammar, detailed in the National Literacy Strategy, can be both observed and crafted into the children's creative narrative writing.

Primary teachers have recently begun to flex their professional muscles, exercise their judgement and make more use of their creative competence. Despite the pressures of tests and prescribed curricula, teachers are aware that to be effective, the literacy curriculum needs a flexible and engaging approach. Such an approach acknowledges the importance of children developing knowledge about language, and highlights the creative application of such naming and knowing. Balancing knowledge about language, which can be measured and tested, and creative language use, which is harder to assess, is essential if we are to motivate and involve young learners.

Children need to develop their knowledge about language and should be supported in making their implicit knowledge explicit, but the development of such knowledge and

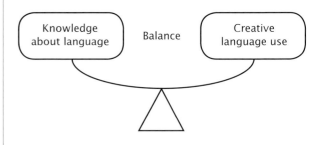

understanding must be offered in a manner that inspires interest and enthusiasm and encourages both the voice of the writer and the views of the reader. A better balance needs to be created in literacy teaching between form and freedom, accuracy and fluency, and structure and innovation – particularly in the area of teaching narrative.

Creative literacy learning

As the OFSTED Report *Successful Primary Schools* makes clear, those schools that raise and sustain standards offer a broad, balanced and creative curriculum (OFSTED, 2003). This is further confirmed by *Excellence and Enjoyment*, the government's current strategy for primary schools (DfES, 2003).

This series of three books on creatively teaching story elements across the primary years responds to the requirements of the National Curriculum, as well as the recommendations in the National Literacy Strategy, in a creative and flexible manner. The books are based on the belief that effective teachers of literacy are informed and creative teachers of literacy; teachers who build strong relationships have considerable knowledge about language, literature and learning and are both responsive to learners' needs and able to inspire and motivate children. Such teachers create imaginative contexts for purposeful literacy use, as well as employing direct instruction when appropriate.

The wealth of interactive activities offered in this book is intended to support teachers in developing open-ended, yet focused approaches to narrative. *Creative Activities for Plot, Character and Setting: Ages 7–9* also offers activity ideas that can be employed with 9 to 11 year olds. There are, however, no formulae here, no panaceas for short story writing, but a bias towards the innovative is evident, and exploration and imaginative engagement are actively encouraged. The focus is on investigating features of fiction 'from the inside out' to complement and energise the explicit study of narrative elements. Teachers are invited to experiment with the activities, to take a full part in them, responding to their learners and adapting the ideas in action. In developing more creative approaches, teachers will be involved in the generation and application of ideas, understanding and knowledge about narrative.

The range of possible narratives

At this age, children will be meeting a variety of narratives outside school, through conversations, television, the cinema, video games, graphic novels, electronic books, CD-ROMs, comics and magazines. The texts they encounter in school need to be high-quality examples of the best available and need to be enriched by examples from other forms, such as television and comics. In the National Literacy Strategy, the fiction listed for these years includes: stories by significant children's writers; traditional stories; myths legends, and fables from a range of cultures; novels and stories from a range of cultures and traditions; classic fiction; adaptations of classics on film and television; longer established stories and novels from more than one genre; and comparison of work by the same author or different authors' treatment of the same theme. Almost any text a teacher wanted to share with her class across this time could fit this wide brief, and this is important since teachers need to feel free to choose books they know, like and perceive will work for their class.

Knowledge of literature is central to the learning strategies and activities described in this book and many different kinds of text can be used to teach narrative elements. Picture fiction and traditional tales tend to be the easiest and most effective to use as they often model the characteristic features of fiction clearly and in a manner that encourages observation and imitation. In novels, the complexity of the plot and the gradual development of subtle characters can make it very difficult to use such stories as models for writing narratives. In addition, multi-modal texts, such as picture books or oral stories, which use more than one mode to communicate their meaning, are the norm in children's worlds and need to be recognised and valued in the classroom. Children in upper Key Stage 2 find such texts very appealing and many are extremely demanding, well written and multi-layered, offering plenty of opportunities for inference and deduction. Most significantly however, children are expected to write short stories and so need extensive experience of short stories in picture books and anthologies as these provide the most appropriate models for writing.

© Derek Cooknell

Much picture fiction is aimed at older readers and mustn't be perceived as 'babyish' by staff or children, for it can provide excellent examples of well-structured short narratives and engage readers/learners through visual images. Teachers who tend not to use such books with older learners are often surprised at the involvement and motivation of the children and come to realise the books' potential. Such books connect to the visual world of television, cinema film and computer games and will utilise and draw upon the children's competence as visually literate people.

With each activity, suggestions are made for literature links. These encompass texts suitable for study at this age and suitable for the activity, and prioritise picture fiction and traditional tales but also include short stories and novels. Teachers will know many other books and videos which might suit the particular activity and engage their learners. To honour the text and the children's interests, tailored text extracts read out of context must at all costs be avoided, but in a unit of work on significant authors, shorter versions can be studied and longer novels read aloud. Equally, well structured chapters or passages can be chosen from the class novel for contextualised study. The chosen narrative needs to be both powerful and enticing to support the motivated involvement and imaginative engagement of the children.

Integrating reading, writing, speaking and listening

The significance of all three modes of language operating in harmony needs to be recognised and can be made a working reality in the classroom. Children need time to talk about texts to make sense of them; such talk will be before, during and after writing, as this can help young writers communicate more effectively. With so many detailed teaching objectives to cover and with the added pressure of written tests, talk is often short-changed if teachers are not very careful.

Teacher Training Agency research shows that effective teachers of literacy profile the meanings of stories and set the teaching of word-, text- and sentence-level skills in the context of powerful narratives that appeal to children (*Teaching Literacy Effectively in the Primary School* by David Wray and Jane Medwell, Routledge). The activities suggested therefore need to be integrated into units of work, since they cannot on their own enable richer learning about narrative elements. For example, in a unit of work on traditional tales, Stories to tell could be used. Several of the activities could be used across a three or four week block to involve the children imaginatively and support their understanding of one or more narrative elements. The National Literacy Strategy text-level objectives for these years, in relation to reading and writing narrative, cover the full range of story elements including understanding aspects of narrative structure, such as how authors handle time. They also consider how film and books can be compared in relation to setting or characters to explore character perspective and viewpoint, to write in the style of the author and to explore the differences and similarities between oral and written retellings.

The objectives in the new guidelines *Speaking, Listening, Learning: working with children* are well covered in the activities, with plenty of opportunities for speaking and listening in pairs, small group discussion of texts and a range of drama activities to bring text to life. Talk is woven through all the narrative activities suggested, many of which suit shared reading or writing and can be used to support independent reading and/or writing. Some describe a reading-focused, discursive activity, although writing possibilities may emerge as the activity is undertaken. Development possibilities are also suggested which teachers can select from, shape and transform in interaction with their children. The series aims to support the imaginative teaching of narrative elements, enabling children to learn through creative involvement with the meaning of texts.

Chapter One

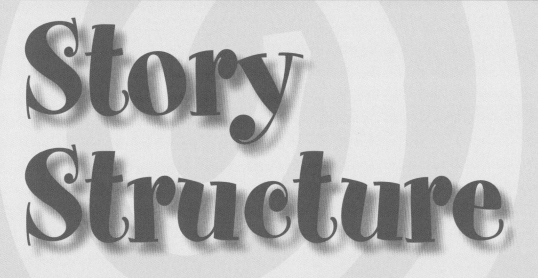

Story Structure

Story structures of all kinds need to be examined, discussed, experienced and constructed in the classroom. In order to observe and make use of narrative structures, children need to meet a wealth of well-structured short stories, in which the development of narrative structure is extremely clear. These can operate as explicit models for children's own narrative writing.

On this journey from the deconstruction of a tale to the construction of a new one, the spoken word plays a critical role. Children need to hear such narratives read aloud. They need to tell and retell stories and find ways to represent particular structures so that they are retained for later use. This will involve them in drawing, talking, improvising and re-creating scenes, both symbolically and literally. In actively voicing stories and retelling tales, they will experience the verbal patterning and emotive journey of the narrative. So, many of the following activities involve opportunities for oral storytelling that follows on from a structural investigation. In this way, the structure of various tales can be internalised over time.

The National Literacy Strategy profiles aspects of narrative structure for children aged 9 to 11, and highlights the use of literary models. Good, clear models are essential in supporting children's awareness of story structure, since different versions of the same tale can be explored, conflicts and build-ups considered, and flashbacks and flash-forwards in time identified. Various story structures can be explored with the class and over time, teachers can list other texts or chapters that follow similar plot patterns. Examples of these structural types are listed below. Story structures can be a useful focus for a unit of work, using displays of texts with the given structure and giving children opportunities to hear, read, tell and write their own tales with a similar structure.

Problem-resolution tales

These often present a clear difficulty at the start of the narrative then a series of steps are taken by the protagonist(s) to resolve this difficulty. The problem is finally resolved, often by ingenious means, at the close of the tale. See, for example, *Catkin* by Antonia Barber (Walker Books), *The Boy and the Cloth of Dreams* by Jenny Koralek (Walker Books), 'The Jester and the King' (page 82) and 'The Old Woman in the Wood' (page 94).

Journey tales

These stories often involve the main character coming across a series of people, animals or places on a clearly identifiable journey. Sometimes, the character returns home enriched by the experience, as in *Way Home* by Libby Hathorn (Red Fox), *Angus Rides the Goods Train* by Alan Durant (Picture Corgi) and 'The Weaving of a Dream' (page 84 of this book). In other stories, the characters remain in their new setting, so the narratives are one-way journeys, for example *The Steadfast Tin Soldier* by Hans Christian Andersen (a lovely version is illustrated by PJ Lynch, Andersen Press) and *The Great Escape* by Philippe Dupasquier (Walker Books). The narrative order varies in these stories, but often encompasses a variation on: introduction – build-up – climaxes or conflicts – resolutions.

Cumulative tales

These tales often include a series of events or the introduction of characters at regular intervals as the narrative grows cumulatively. Towards the close of the story, something tends to happen that explodes the situation or drastically changes the status quo. Cumulative stories include classics such as 'The Enormous Turnip', and examples can also be found in modern picture books, such as *The Tower to the Sun* by Colin Thompson and *The Dog That Dug* by Jonathan Long (both Red Fox).

Climactic tales

Climactic stories often have a marked crescendo and an explosive climax, after which the characters return home or the story comes to an end. Chapters are very often left on a climax or cliffhanger, as in the *Afterdark* series by Annie Dalton, and in Lemony Snicket's *A Series of Unfortunate Events*.

The activities described in this chapter seek to bring narrative structures to life; to help children notice the construction of the plot, identify the key incidents, understand the sequenced stages of a tale's telling and notice the techniques authors use to indicate the passing of time. These features can usefully be used as a mirror for writing.

© Photodisc, Inc.

Skeleton summaries

This activity describes the backbone or main structure of a story in a skeleton outline that emphasises the significant events or key words in the narrative. This resumé can then be used to retell part of the story orally, focusing on a climatic moment, or a section of particular interest, personal significance or connection. The activity enables children to summarise a story in less than 50 words and identify the key stages of a story's telling. The skeleton summary is a form of note taking of the story outline and can be used to show the narrative's structure and development.

What to do

❶ Read or tell a highly structured traditional tale that the children don't already know, for example 'The Jester and the King' (page 82).

❷ Ask the children to work in pairs to identify the simple beginning, middle and end of the story. While they are discussing this, draw a large skeleton on the board.

❸ Through whole class discussion, establish the three parts of the story and encourage the children to provide summary statements/shorthand notes that represent the skeleton's head (beginning), its torso and arms (middle) and down its legs (end). These statements are in effect subheadings, for example:

- *Jester too old – dismissed* (beginning)
- *Poor and hungry; tricks queen and tricks king* (middle)
- *Lives contentedly* (end).

❹ Focusing on the start of the story, model the process of generating key words and phrases to summarise the section under the subheading *Jester too old – dismissed*. These could be a bulleted list of the key

Literature Links

This activity needs texts with an overt narrative structure, such as traditional tales like 'The Weaving of a Dream' (page 84), 'The Call of the Sea' (page 88) or 'The Old Woman in the Wood' (page 94). Another example is *Ladder to the Sky* by Barbara Esbensen (Little, Brown). Chaptered books also work well if only one well-shaped chapter is used as the basis of the activity, for example any of *The Dream Master* trilogy by Theresa Breslin or *I Was a Rat!* by Philip Pullman (both Yearling). Some short stories collections are useful, such as Philippa Pearce's *The Rope and Other Stories* (Puffin). The activity works best with a text that the children do not know very well.

Page 9

events to be agreed on and written in the head of the skeleton, for example:

- Royal jester, laughter
- Age creeps on
- King and queen despair
- Jester forcibly 'retired'

These notes act as written triggers to recall the detail of the text. Stress to the children that each of the words chosen has to represent many others, so long descriptions are not appropriate and brevity and precision is required. To emphasise this, take one of the bullet points, for example *Age creeps on*. Retell or re-read that part of the story, demonstrating to the children that this simple statement encompasses quite a lot and could have been expanded to include more detail, for example *Sometimes Matenko fell as he skipped, sometimes he forgot the punch lines of his jokes.*

⑤ Give out photocopies of a skeleton shape so that each pair of children has one between them. Ask the pairs to record their own bullet point summaries in the middle section (torso and pelvis) of the skeleton. Encourage them to discuss and agree on the precise wording for each point before they write anything down. They will have to write very neatly and in small handwriting, but this all helps to encourage economy with words. Each bullet point could represent a paragraph or section of the story.

⑥ Record some ideas in the main skeleton shape on the board. Ask the children to vote on two or three examples, discussing which few words convey the most.

⑦ Now move on to agreeing together on the bullet point summaries in the final section – the legs, for example:

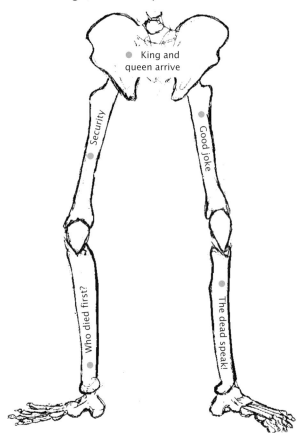

- King and queen arrive

Security

Good joke

Who died first?

The dead speak!

With the children, count the total number of words used in the class example of the whole story. If it is over 50, work together to try to reduce the total to 50 words or fewer. Explain to the children that you have together created a story summary that does not retell the tale, but encompasses the key events through the three subheadings and the bullet points of narrative action.

⑧ Invite the children in pairs to select one part of the tale – the beginning, the middle or the end – and use the bullet points to retell this orally to their partners. Encourage them to add flesh to the bare bones of the story as they tell it.

⑨ Then invite the pairs to help each other share one paragraph of their oral retelling with the class.

⑩ The pairs can write out this paragraph, working individually or together.

© Derek Cooknell

STORY
SKELETON

Hunter's
Five sons

Hunter - Weapons - Woods

Weep 1 2 3

forgotten week 4

baby "where's my dad?"

dad - Skeleton

I have 2 flesh 3 life 4 moths
dad carve
2 mths
mine x 5!
baby given it for - remember
dad
The
End.

The moral to this
Story is even if
someone is dead,
they are still alive
if you remember them
in your
heart.

Moving on

● Encourage the children to find a highly structured traditional tale to retell. They could create their own skeleton summary as a way of summarising the structure and adding it to their story memory, prior to retelling it orally and/or rewriting one paragraph.

● Children can use skeleton summaries as plans for their own stories, working towards summarising their story in less than 50 words and using the bullet points as markers for paragraphs to be fleshed out in the next stage of writing.

● Focus on the style of the telling, for example short and humorous, lyrical and poetic, descriptive. Discuss how the children could 'dress' their skeleton appropriately. For example, if it is a short, funny story, they could add shorts, a T-shirt and sunglasses to the skeleton. If the tale is more descriptive, decorative and 'old fashioned', perhaps ruffles, cuffs, buckles and frills would suit. You could refer to this dress style with stories you read in the future. This can become a useful metaphor.

Creative Activities for Plot, Character & Setting: Ages 9-11

Problem solving

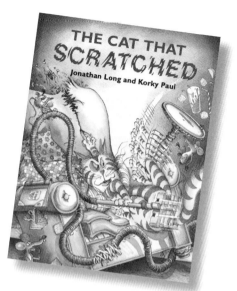

The purpose of this activity is to deepen the children's understanding of how events in some stories are structured, in particular, problem-resolution stories with a simple framework. It also creates opportunities for children to extend their ideas using the simple framework in a predictable and humorous story. The use of picture fiction for this purpose is particularly appropriate, as the stories can normally be read in a single session and tend to be sufficiently fantastic to allow risks to be taken with the imagination, with little opportunity for failure. The skills practised within this genre can then be transferred to the exploration of novels and extended texts.

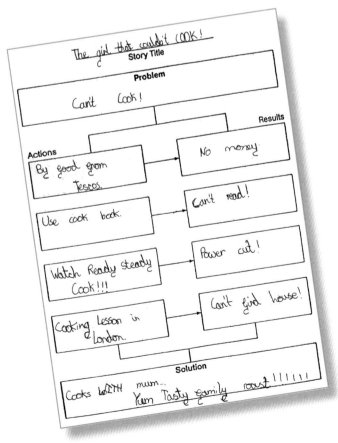

Literature links

Stories that will be suitable for this activity need to have a clear and predictable structure that can easily be identified as a formula of action and resolution, for example *The Cat that Scratched* and *The Dog that Dug* by Jonathan Long (Red Fox), *The Rascally Cake* by Jeanne Willis (Puffin), *Angry Arthur* by Hiawyn Oram (Red Fox), or slightly longer texts, such as *Rats!* by Pat Hutchins (Red Fox) or *The Owl Who Was Afraid of the Dark* by Jill Tomlinson (Mammoth). *How to Write Really Badly* by Anne Fine (Egmont) is a more subtle story that could be used to inspire a range of different resolutions.

What to do

❶ Read *The Cat that Scratched* by Jonathan Long, or another story that is structured on a series of problems and resolutions.

❷ Allow some time for personal responses and intertextual connections to be made and inferences and implications drawn. Say to the children, for example: *Turn to the person next to you and tell them three things you liked about the story* or, *Name a story with a similar structure* and so on. Then briefly discuss these responses as a class.

③ In a shared or guided writing session, show the children the following diagram in the middle of the board:

Title
The Cat That Scratched

Problem
The cat has fleas

Action ⟶ Result

Action ⟶ Result

Action ⟶ Result

Solution

Encourage the children to retell the story with you and systematically reconstruct the structure by agreeing on the central, or opening, problem, noting the various actions that follow and the results of these, culminating in the closing solution to the problem and the end of the tale.

④ In pairs, ask the children to work to construct their own diagram and then use it to retell the story collaboratively to another pair.

⑤ Share and compare these versions of the story. Do they differ significantly?

⑥ This type of diagram is useful for the children to help them understand the structure of stories and to use when they are constructing their own. The children could be asked to think of a problem for a simple story (*Aunty is coming to tea today and I need to serve a cake*) and a number of ways of solving it (*Buying a cake, Using a recipe, Asking Mum to make one*). They then think of incidents or circumstances that may prevent these occurring (*It's Sunday and the shops are closed. All the recipe books have been donated to the school fête. Mum has to go to work*) and a

© Derek Cooknell

final solution (*A neighbour has had a baking day and can't fit all of her cakes in her freezer!*). Model this with the children on the first occasion, as this will be helpful to them. They could then work on deciding on a problem and resolving it in the required number of steps.

Moving on

● This structure could be further developed by inviting the children, in guided writing activities, to extend this frame and enhance it. For example, there could be more than one problem to contend with, generating two 'branches' to a diagram.

● Ask the children to work in pairs, with one partner inventing a problem for a story and the other suggesting the resolutions. The partners could then swap roles before choosing which of the diagrams would be suitable for shaping and developing into a fully fledged story.

Story possibilities

In this activity, the children make connections between visual images generated by a story and construct a story plot from them. The activity is an effective precursor to reading a text as a class novel or short story and encourages the use of hypothesis and prediction, anticipation and imagination. It involves the whole class in projecting possibilities and making interpretations, and invites them to engage with the story prior to you reading it. The activity can also encourage an examination of the similarities and differences between oral and written storytelling.

Literature links

Any text can be used for this activity, but this is a particularly useful way into a long novel, as it sets up expectations and predictions that will only be answered by close attention to the text over time. You will need to know the novel well enough to identify relevant elements. Suggestions include *I, Jack* by Patricia Finney (Yearling), *Holes* by Louis Sachar (Bloomsbury), *How to Write Really Badly* by Anne Fine (Egmont), *The Fire Within* by Chris d'Lacey (Orchard) and *A Bad Beginning* by Lemony Snicket (Egmont). Short stories like 'The Old Woman in the Wood' (page 94) and 'The Weaving of a Dream' (page 84), as well as picture books, such as *The Coming of the Surfman* by Peter Collington (Red Fox) and *A Cultivated Wolf* by Becky Bloom (Siphano), would also work.

What to do

⓵ Select a story you intend to read and study during a unit of work, for example, *Holes* by Louis Sachar. Using clip art, your own drawing skills or visuals from the book, choose around six to ten simple icons to represent significant characters and events in the narrative (see examples below). Position these in random order on an A4 sheet and produce 10 copies for the children.

2. Explain to the children that their challenge is to solve the mystery and create a range of possibilities. They are to identify images from the story and seek to create connections to construct a possible narrative. Don't show them the book or give them the title of the story.

3. Organise the children into groups of four and let them number themselves individually (1 to 4) in each group. Ask all the number 3s, for example, to come to you and give them a few seconds to look carefully at the sheet with the picture clues about the narrative. Tell them to return to their group and, on a large sheet of paper, draw one of the items they have seen. Challenge the group to start thinking of a story or an event that surrounds the image.

4. Call out the other numbers in turn, until all the images have been transferred to the groups' sheets. Allow time for observation, drawing and discussion. More time for discussion will be needed as the number of images that the groups collect increases. Stress that the images are shown and copied in no particular order. Explain to the children that after each image has been added, the group should try to make further connections between the pictures to create a story structure.

5. When all visuals have been transferred, allow groups some time to firm up their proposed narrative. Make it clear that they will be telling this story to others, so suggest they explicitly identify significant events, key characters or problems and resolutions. You may want to provide a frame to include who the key characters are, where the tale is set, what key events happen and whether a resolution or ending is possible to predict. After they have done this, give a copy of the original A4 sheet to each group, so that they can compare their pictures. It may be that they have 'misinterpreted' certain visuals; this

doesn't really matter, as they will have made up their own story with their own remembered visuals.

6. Ask each group to tell their story to the class, using their story possibility sheets. Avoid using the writing frame at this stage, as this will lead to reporting rather than narrating.

7. As a class, discuss any differences in representation. For example, a group may have mistaken the lizard for a snake – what differences did this make to their proposed story structure?

8. Discuss which story the children preferred and what their starting point was. Was it the characters or the setting? It is likely to have been the interaction between the narrative elements, when *action* occurred, for example when one of the characters shot a lizard or became stranded in the desert.

9. Later, when you read the title of the original story and begin reading the text, refer to the children's predictions and discuss differences and similarities.

Moving on

● Ask the children to divide up their story and select one aspect each to write up in a paragraph. This will be best if undertaken in narrative order, with the first writer passing on the story to the second and so on. It could become a group homework task over a week.

● Invite the children to create the title and the blurb that might appear on the back of the book, using the limited knowledge they have and their hypotheses hinting at story structure. They could work in pairs or in their original groups. Share these examples and discuss how the character and setting influenced the narrative action.

Timelines

This activity invites children to create, in diagrammatic form, the structure of a story they know. By doing so, they begin to see how stories are formed chronologically and how elements in a story's structure are intrinsically linked. The timeline that the children create can then be used as a planning device when they come to write their own stories. This activity explicitly connects children's own plans for story writing with the insights and knowledge gained from working with the stories of others. Many great writers of the past have borrowed structures from older tales when making their new ones; this activity enables young writers to learn in the same way. A timeline is a useful tool for plotting the significant events in a story.

What to do

❶ Before reading the story with the children, make sure you have a good memory of the significant events (and the number of them) so you can choose the best format for the timeline (for example, portrait or landscape; sentence annotations or captioned pictures).

Literature links

Timelines can be drawn up for a wealth of different stories, videos or the class novel. Traditional tales provide very clear story structures that can be used well to support this activity, for example 'The Old Woman in the Wood' (page 94) and 'George and the Dragon' (page 92). Fairy stories with a difference can be found in *Fairy Tales* and *Fantastic Stories* by Terry Jones (both Penguin). Folk tales about the

❷ Read a story that will engage the children. 'The Old Woman in the Wood' (page 94) is a terrific tale to tell and has a clear structure that will help this activity. As you read, try to use exaggerated facial expressions, dramatic pauses, movement and actions to help keep the children involved in the story.

❸ Then, as a shared activity, invite the children to help you construct a timeline for the events of the story on the board. (It is up to you whether the basic line is vertical or horizontal, and this may

moon from around the world can be found in *Moon Tales* by Rina Singh (Bloomsbury). Longer stories with a more complicated plot and structure like *Charlotte's Web* by EB White (Puffin) or Philip Pullman's *His Dark Materials* novels (Scholastic) can also be perfect for the timeline summary.

Timeline of events from 'The Old Woman in the Wood'

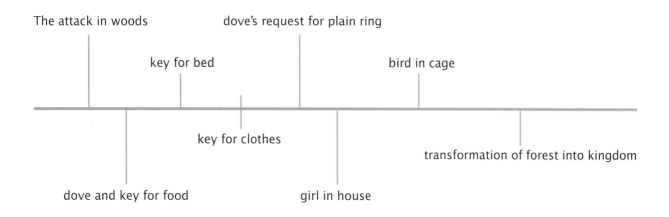

depend on the number of significant events and how they are to be marked.) You may want to choose just the beginning of the story and allow the children to work in pairs to complete the rest. Remember to think aloud as you write, and utilise the children's ideas to chart the chronological progress of the story. Prompt them with questions such as, *What is the first significant moment of the story? What shall we write to help us remember? What important event happens next?* Write short sentences or shorthand phrases that describe each point of the story the class wishes to highlight on their timeline.

4 The timeline could also be illustrated. Make sure the children understand that you are marking significant events from the story on the timeline (through sentences or pictures), and that you are marking them *in chronological order.*

5 Once the timeline has been made with the important events of the story plotted and annotated, you could work together to retell the story using the timeline, or the children could reproduce the timeline themselves on an A3 sheet, and use it to retell the story orally to each other in pairs. It would be interesting to spend a few minutes comparing the versions.

Moving on

● The children could work in pairs to plot chronologically the events of another story they know well or have recently read, writing a brief annotation and/or drawing a simple picture to explain each event they mark. Again, encourage them then to use the timeline to support an oral retelling of the story to another group of children or another class.

● Children can draw a timeline of the class novel in their reading journals, extending and developing this on a daily basis. You might want to encourage them, in this instance, to note their personal responses to the events as they go along.

● Encourage the children to use the idea of the timeline to plan their own stories before writing. Plotting the important events from start to finish before setting out to write will help a writer to take an overview of their story structure, in terms of narrative incident, timescale, excitement, coherence and so on. To give real purpose to the writing, tell the children that their stories will be compiled in a book for the class library, and suggest that they design them and add pictures using a desktop publishing package.

Coming soon...

The purpose of this activity is to help children to review the work of some established authors, to acknowledge and articulate what is special about their work and to write discursively about a novel or story by a familiar author. By this stage of their primary education, children are likely to have gathered a repertoire of familiar and favourite stories and authors. They will already be experienced in browsing in book collections. Sometimes the choice is made intuitively, with little attempt to categorise the text or analyse the reason for the choice. For this activity, the children need to become familiar with the work of a bank of authors and be able to summarise their themes and approaches. There is an opportunity to enjoy the excitement and anticipation around a new title about to come out. As well as using publicity material, you could introduce the children to book reviews in newspapers and magazines.

What to do

1. In shared reading time, show the children the front and back covers of a new or unfamiliar text by a familiar author. (If possible, use ICT to enlarge the visual image and the text on the covers.) Try to create a sense of drama and anticipation around this part of the activity to ensure the engagement of all the children. For example, suggest that the book cannot be opened as it has been sealed to avoid pre-publication 'leaks' about its contents (this could be described in different ways, depending on the age and experience of the children) and any information about the story must be gleaned from the clues offered on the covers.

2. Gather and share all this information, for example, during a brainstorm. Encourage the children to locate the publisher's logo, title, author, illustrator, the blurb on the back, and to read review information and

Literature links

For this activity, it would be useful to begin with unfamiliar picture fiction, but by a familiar author, that can be read in a single session and easily characterised. The children would then be able to progress to short novels or stories by well-known authors from which they can draw comparisons and make predictions. For example, to begin, the humorous work of Anthony Browne in *Changes* (Walker Books), or Lauren Child in any of the Clarice Bean stories (Orchard) would be engaging to work with and may attract the attention of inexperienced or disaffected readers. Move on to authors such as Lemony Snicket, JK Rowling, Berlie Doherty, who writes in a particular style in, for example

Street Child (Lions) and *Daughter of the Sea* (Puffin), and Jacqueline Wilson in *The Illustrated Mum* (Yearling) or Anne Fine in *Step by Wicked Step* (Puffin). Collect a varied set of books by the same author and other books with which to make comparisons. If possible, try to obtain cover proofs, advertising posters or press releases from publishers.

any other written text offered. Use this opportunity to look at publicity material and reviews.

❸ Ask the children to work in pairs to predict a) what the book may be about – the content, b) the genre and c) the tone – humorous, informative and so on. Ask them to draw up a list of notes or brief bullet-pointed statements at this stage. Support these predictions by urging the children to use their knowledge of the author's style, genre and so on to make informed comments. Prompt them to make connections with other books they have read or books in the class collection.

❹ Share these predictions and observations, and come to some conclusions, still without 'checking' in the story itself. In shared writing, compose these into a blurb.

❺ The story book could be made inaccessible by sealing it with a paper band, or placing it in a transparent pocket. It could then be pinned high on the wall until the end of the day, or, indeed the end of the week, in order to maintain the suspense and wonder. Alternatively, display the publishers' cover proofs and publicity material.

❻ At the end of the session, day or week, reveal to the children that you have received an advance copy of the book or have just bought one from a bookshop (include the carrier bag). Share the book to enable the children to see which of their constructed 'blurbs' are close to the intentions of the author. Discuss the differences. Which do the children prefer? Is the story 'typical' of this author?

❼ Add the children's suggested blurbs to the publicity display.

© Clynt Garnham

Moving on

● The technique learned in this activity could be further developed by reversing the procedure. The children could read a story then provide the information to create an exciting and enthusiastic blurb for the book, describing, explaining or commenting on content, style and impact.

● The children could write a blurb for a certain audience, for example, they could create an exciting cover and informative blurb for a story, to attract the attention of younger children in the school. This work could take a variety of forms, for example a press release (perhaps in the style of the recent Harry Potter articles), a poster, a book jacket or review.

● If the children's anticipated stories are different from the book, encourage the children to write a section of their version of the story, perhaps writing in the style of the author.

Improvise the action

In this drama activity children discuss and then generate possible actions in a story. These could be flashbacks into the past, additional narrative actions, or flash-forwards into the future of the story. This supports children when their own story writing uses flashbacks or a story within a story to convey the passing of time. It helps them to see the ways in which, as authors, they can handle time. Writing that follows on from the drama can be from different points of view and in a variety of genres. The class can then explore how the genre and the viewpoint affect the information shared.

What to do

❶ Select a moment in your class novel that is unknown, for example one that has not yet been read, one that has been mentioned in passing but with little detail, or one that is only referred to by the text. For example, in *Holes* by Louis Sachar, Stanley Yelnats is sent down by the judge, but his crime is not described.

❷ Read up to the appropriate moment and invite groups of children to prepare an improvisation, perhaps of the scene that depicts Stanley's crime. This will create an improvised flashback for the text.

Literature links

This activity works well with almost any type of story, but the selection of a tense moment or situation to improvise is crucial. For example, in *A Bad Beginning* by Lemony Snicket (Egmont) when the Baudelaire Orphans arrive on the doorstep of Count Olaf's strange house, what might happen when Mr Po leaves? Or in *The Wreck of the Zanzibar* by Michael Morpurgo (Egmont), what adventures might befall Billy as he follows Hannibal to sail the seas? One unfortunate incident could be improvised which makes Billy wonder whether he made the right decision to leave Bryher. In *Saffy's Angel* by Hilary McKay (Hodder & Stoughton), what happens when she is discovered as a stowaway to Italy in the back of her friends' parents' car? In *The Wretched Stone* by Chris van Allsburg (Houghton Mifflin), what is it that the sailors find on the enchanted island? In *Holes* by Louis Sachar (Bloomsbury), the children could improvise the crime Stanley Yelnats is supposed to have committed. All opportunities to improvise possible action need to be open-ended, indicating unknown events, or as flash-forwards or flashbacks in the text.

③ Provide time for discussion about this unknown scene, then create a class rehearsal of the scene: ask all the groups to practise their scene simultaneously as a practice, prior to sharing extracts from them one at a time.

④ Ask the groups to select one crucial moment in their scene to show as a freeze-frame or still picture of that moment, for example, the moment Stanley was caught in *Holes*, the moment he stole a purse or the moment his friends deserted him as the police arrived.

⑤ When these are chosen, suggest that the image of the freeze-frame was photographed by the press and appeared on the front page of the local newspaper. Ask the groups to consider what headline might have accompanied it, for example *Young thief caught at last, Yelnats strikes again, Teenagers terrorise the neighbourhood*. In effect, the groups are titling their freeze-frames, which act as a summary of their improvisations.

⑥ As a class, see each freeze-frame in turn and hear the headlines, inviting elaboration where necessary.

⑦ Ask the children to write the news article for their headline. You may want to work on one in shared writing first. Remind them to make use of typical newspaper text attributes such as subheadings, a byline, straplines and reported speech from eyewitnesses interviewed at the scene.

© Derek Cooknell

Moving on

● Create another improvisation from the same text. For example, suggest that after Stanley arrived at the detention centre, some journalists arrived. This could be a whole class improvisation with three children as the Warden, Mr Sir and Mr Pendanski, and the rest in role as journalists or suspicious members of the NSPCC. A variety of opportunities for writing in role could develop from this, for example news reports, magazine articles, diary entries and camp log records.

● Improvise a range of alternative possible narrative actions to demonstrate the potential variety. The class could brainstorm a list of significant narrative happenings that could follow the one you are focusing on, and then select one per group to create. For example, in 'The Weaving of a Dream' (page 84), what might happen when Leje reached the palace where his mother's woven tapestry had been taken? Such an activity helpfully demonstrates the variety of possible options, the choices authors make and the validity of interpretations.

The dog's tail

This activity focuses on the relationship between the beginnings and endings of overtly shaped short stories. It highlights the potential connection between the opening lines or paragraph and the final lines. A story's narrative is likened to the body of a dog, with the dog's head being the beginning (the opening lines its nose), its main body the middle and the dog's bottom representing the end of the tale. This metaphor is extended to focus on the dog's tail (the very last paragraph or line), which often reaches round and touches (connects with) the dog's nose (the first paragraph or line). With practice, this activity can help children create more coherent narratives with evident linguistic shape and related content, and threads that connect the opening with the closing of the tale, giving a satisfying rounded structure.

Literature links

The most useful text models for this activity are those narratives that adroitly revisit the language of the opening at their close. For example:

- *Red Eyes at Night* – Michael Morpurgo (Hodder)
- *Sharon and Darren* – Nigel Gray (Young Lions)
- *Gorilla* – Anthony Browne (Walker Books)
- *Rats!* – Pat Hutchins (Red Fox).

Many other texts also have 'dog's tails' that wag round – these will be easiest to notice in short story collections, picture books and short novels.

What to do

❶ Read an example of a story with a dog's tail in it and ask the children to listen particularly carefully to the beginning and the end of the tale. This is where picture books can come into their own, as they are short enough to read in one sitting. If you are using a novel, complete the book, then re-read the opening and closing paragraphs to begin this activity.

❷ Highlight the connections between the opening and closing statements. Re-read these paragraphs or lines, making inferences and deductions together if the children don't know the story.

❸ Show the children a large picture of a dog you have drawn, or ask a child to draw one, and explain how the dog's body represents different parts of the story. Highlight the dog's nose and indicate how the tail can be made to wag and touch the nose if the author chooses to revisit the first lines as in the example you recorded on the board. Re-read the example together to demonstrate this.

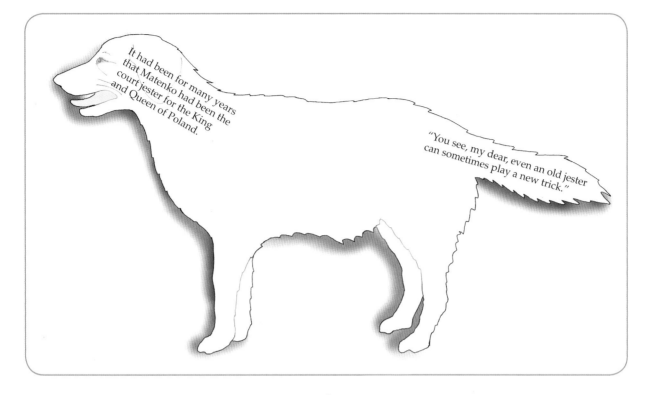

It had been for many years that Matenko had been the court jester for the King and Queen of Poland.

"You see, my dear, even an old jester can sometimes play a new trick."

❹ Share some other examples, preferably from stories the children know. These could be from very simple tales, including picture books, that are not necessarily taxing for this age group. What matters is that they contain obvious dog's noses and tails that wag! Discuss how the story's theme or problem is made clear in the opening and resolved by the end.

❺ Provide children with strips of paper (an A4 sheet cut in half vertically works well) and invite them to create their own dog's noses, writing only the beginning of a possible tale on the strip. Emphasise that merely the first few lines or the opening paragraph is required.

❻ Drop these dog noses into a hat or box and encourage the children to take out one each. Then, working in pairs, ask the children to take it in turns to read the opening to their partner. Together they should project each of the possible narratives and agree a viable dog's tail. The lines that represent the tail should be written on the back of the strip.

❼ Encourage the children to share some of their nose and wagging tail examples in a plenary session. Celebrate their success, discussing the ways in which the connecting threads may have been achieved, for example through problem resolution, repetition, time, reflection upon a character's former state and so on.

Moving on

● Display these noses and tails as mobiles. Give time for the children to read them, then invite them to write the middle of a chosen story, framed by the nose and tail.

● Set up a dog's tail hunt and invite the children, over a fortnight in a unit of work highlighting story structure, to identify and record in their reading journals examples of rounded and connecting openings and endings.

● Make a large wall display of a dog with extracts in numerous noses and wagging tails, perhaps with ribbon connecting to the books in question, so that the children can read more from the examples available.

Parallel plots

Children at this age are ready to explore stories in a sophisticated and analytical manner. They should be encouraged to look for subtleties and depth and uncover the polysemic nature of what may appear to be a simple text. Using the work of skilful authors and illustrators, the children will be supported in constructing layers of narrative in their story writing. This activity gives children the opportunity to develop a sophisticated idea of the nature of story structure, identifying parallel stories in known texts and using this model in a story structure of their own. The activity will also allow them to investigate different versions of the same story in print and/or film, identifying and discussing similarities and differences.

What to do

❶ Stories as described above could be read and importantly *shown* to the children as a model for their own writing. The visual nature of some of these texts is very significant.

❷ Discuss some potential ideas for presenting two parallel stories, for example in the Dupasquier style of split pages, John Burningham's style of generating two stories through separate written and pictorial texts and Michael Morpurgo's structure of using Laura's diary and then Billy's adventures to create parallel structures in the *Wreck of the Zanzibar* (Egmont). He does this again effectively, but across time, in *Farm Boy* (Collins).

Literature links

Some very talented authors and illustrators use this parallel story structure very effectively. For example, the work of Philippe Dupasquier in *Dear Daddy* (Longman) and *A Country Far Away* (Orchard) makes the two different perspectives very visible. John Burningham's *Come Away From the Water, Shirley* (Red Fox) again offers dual perspectives and would help children at this stage of development in deconstructing the methods and messages of the author/illustrator. To extend this activity, look at the way that film also achieves this, particularly in stories such as *Goodnight Mister Tom* by Michelle Magorian (Puffin), which has been filmed for television. As children progress in this way of investigating texts, some of the film versions of Shakespeare's plays will be an achievable challenge for more able readers

and writers. From a reading of, for example, *Come Away From the Water, Shirley*, the children could discuss other contexts in which parents and children have different agendas or experiences. *Not Now, Bernard* by David McKee (Red Fox) would be another apparently simple story containing layers of meaning for children to uncover.

From *Dear Daddy* © Philippe Dupasquier (Andersen Press)

❸ Organise the children into pairs and ask each pair to choose a common theme to develop (a car journey with parents in the front and children in the back might be a simple suggestion useful to start ideas flowing). Explain that they are going to develop their theme into a story with two different tales or perspectives within it. Other examples might be of two boys playing football, one actually playing the game, while the other is dressed in team kit but dreaming at home. Another suggestion might be to depict two children of the same age, one at school and the other (for a reason chosen by the children) at home, and show the differences in their day.

❹ Initially, tell the children to use a storyboard approach to plan out their story. Remind them of comic strips that they are familiar with, or frames from *Dear Daddy*. Encourage the children to think of each part of the story as a separate scene. It can then be used to compare with the parallel story. Initially it may help the children if they compare one scene at a time, although more experienced writers may want to complete one 'side' of the story before they begin the other. Encourage them to think in frames and to consider life 'outside the box' as well as within it. Encourage the children to think of pairs of scenes.

❺ Now ask the pairs to use the storyboard as a telling prop for the story. Invite some children to perform their story, using two voices for the telling.

Moving on

● In guided sessions, the children's storyboard stories could be further developed. Challenge the children to think of a range of audiences for their stories, from the most inexperienced to adult readers.

● This level of critical appreciation and understanding of authorial subtlety could be extended by getting the children to evaluate ways in which book and film can be used to tell the same story in different ways. Reading the opening pages of *Goodnight Mister Tom* and then viewing the film (Carlton Visual Entertainment, on DVD and video) would provide the children with a starting point for considering their own stories from different perspectives and could make use of the storyboard technique.

● This could be further developed through the use of other filmed books, with the children storyboarding from the film the perspectives that they had gathered during a viewing. The children will naturally choose different characters and perspectives and these could be developed in shared and guided reading and writing sessions.

Symbolic summaries

Symbolic summaries are a useful way of recording the structure of one part of a story, in particular the opening. Rather than using detailed pictures, action can be depicted implicitly through a combination of keywords, symbols, initials and signs. The symbols can help to reconstruct the events and feelings in a section of a story and can be used to compare a number of story openings. They enable children to make 'notes' of the story outline as preparation for oral storytelling, and help them analyse how individual paragraphs have been structured. The children can in turn borrow such structures for their own writing. Any significant part of a story or chapter can be summarised symbolically, although it is often useful for children to focus upon the opening frame and perceive how this shapes the narrative that follows. You may find it best to complete this activity over a couple of sessions.

Literature links

Any unfamiliar text with a beginning that immediately introduces the problem and the characters is particularly useful. Examples include 'The Weaving of a Dream' (page 84) as well as other traditional tales such as those of Anansi. The challenging picture books *Catkin* by Antonia Barber (Walker Books) and *Nobody Rides the Unicorn* by Adrian Mitchell (Picture Corgi) offer strong opening scenes, as do various chapters in the novels *The Machine Gunners* by Robert Westall (Macmillan), *The Iron Man* by Ted Hughes (Faber) and *The Demon Headmaster* series by Gillian Cross (OUP). You will also need a well-known story for the first part of the activity.

What to do

❶ In preparation for the main part of the activity, re-read the beginning of a well-known and popular story to the children, for example *The Iron Man* by Ted Hughes. Explain that you are going to try to record the significant narrative moments in the opening of the story, using symbols and trying to avoid words.

❷ Demonstrate the process by drawing simply and symbolically, using letters, silhouetted shapes and signs to convey the essence of the narrative action. For *The Iron Man*, for example, you might draw a simple solid 'stick man' on the top of a cliff, with his eyes like headlamps searching the sea.

Then re-read the first section and include his fall into the ocean, when his arms, legs, ears and head fall off. Again, depict this very simply, using Ted Hughes' oft-repeated word, *Crash!*

Then read on and ask the class how they want to depict the silence:

Peace and quiet

There is no correct version; you are just modelling the process of making a selection of shapes and signs to represent the beginning of the story. Discuss your ideas with the children and invite them to make suggestions to help you.

3. Now read the opening section of the story you have selected to focus upon in this activity. This should be a story which the children do not know already, for example 'The Weaving of a Dream' (page 84).

4. Create a simple symbolic summary of this, beginning with the whole class. Initially, the most significant events need to be identified and represented simply. For example, in 'The Weaving of a Dream', a simple hut with three brothers and mother could be drawn, then the

market and the importance of the painting. Listen to the children's suggestions asking them to explain them with reference to the text. Record the symbols chosen in the order that the narrative is revealed so that the symbols can be used as a retelling aid later.

5. Ask the children to choose the last of the early events and make their own individual drawings of, for instance, the widow weaving for three years. If you are using a picture book, the illustrations may help, but simplicity is the key. For example:

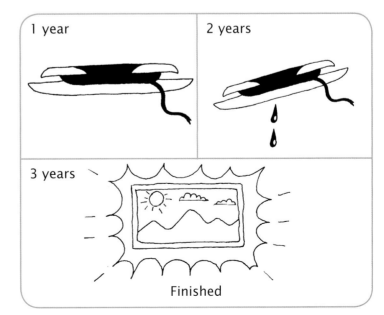

1 year

2 years

3 years

Finished

⑥ Share the children's drawings and discuss which are the most effective – those that are economical in style but representative of the action.

⑦ Now decide as a class how to show the next event, the wind taking the brocade away. Perhaps:

Oh NO!

⑧ Ask pairs of children to use the class symbolic summary, including their own visuals, to retell this opening part of the story. Draw attention to the fact that the symbolic summary has created a resumé of the action so far.

⑨ As a class or in pairs, help the children to write the opening paragraph for the symbolic summary created. Then share these and focus on the use of connectives to create internal cohesion within the paragraph.

⑩ Ask the children to work in their pairs to hypothesise and predict the rest of the tale, making clear the connection to the opening. Then read or tell the whole story and discuss the differences between the children's predictions and the actual tale. Highlight how the opening held the seeds of future action, in that the old woman wove her dream only to lose it as the wind spirited it away.

Moving on

● Encourage the children to use symbolic summaries as starters for their own story writing. Let them select a short story or picture book narrative and create a symbolic summary of its opening, writing the paragraph to go alongside it. These should then be circulated around the class. Allow the children to make selections, then ask them to write the remainder of a story. The original texts can then be made available to the new authors for comparison.

● Create a traditional tale 'quilt', which is a visually interesting way of summarising the children's repertoire following a brainstorm of all the tales they know. Give each child a hexagonal paper shape and suggest that they draw a silhouetted symbol to represent the story in a simple way. 'The Princess and the Pea' might be shown by a tiara and a pea, 'The Stag and the Pool' by a pair of antlers and a pool. These shapes can then be arranged together, and as the children add to their knowledge of such tales, their story quilt grows.

● Create your own symbolic summary for the closure of a story you are reading to the class, without having read the end yet. Offer them your summary, and ask them to write the concluding paragraph based on your symbols.

● Invite the children to identify, copy, collect and display other symbols used in and around the school and home that convey meanings simply. Suggest that they find some that use words and some that don't.

Chapter Two

Characterisation

At this age, children will be familiar with a huge range of complex characters from books and films. They will have seen how characterisation is one of the most influential ingredients of a successful story; they realise how characterisation, in terms of the *type* of characters, influences how events unfold and how the story makes the readers feel.

When audiences read or watch characters behaving in certain ways, carrying out deeds and producing significant events, they will inevitably be forming their own opinions and judgements. Like more mature readers, children will draw on their own values to make these judgements, as well as having their opinions influenced by the events themselves. They will be incensed like Fern in EB White's *Charlotte's Web* when the runt of the litter of pigs is to be killed by her father, or feel a mischievous satisfaction when

Clarice Bean enjoys being sent to her room in Lauren Child's *Clarice Bean, That's Me*. Children make analogies with people and events in their own lives, and this will enrich their understanding of characters in stories.

This is how teaching about character begins; with children's own experiences and intuitive thoughts and feelings. All their views will be valid and worthy of discussion. As a teacher you are charged with assisting children in making their arguments strong. You will need to model how critical readers approach a text, how to infer from what the writer gives to the reader in text and construct their own meanings from this material. In doing this, you will promote an active engagement with the text – an engagement that will bring great joy for the children in later years.

A strength of the National Literacy Strategy is that it encourages teachers to immerse children in specific forms of real story narratives, written by some superb writers. Children can be given time to explore different types of stories and immerse themselves in the worlds of the stories and the characters that inhabit those worlds. Gaining fuller understanding of characters will include the need for children to engage in role-play and dramas. In this way, the characters come off the page and to life in the classroom. Drama will enable children to 'become' the characters in, for example, hot-seat situations and other dramas that can come quite naturally from the books that are being read in class at the time.

Teachers that plan units of work involving teaching certain genres over a two to three week period will then be able to make links between the reading and the writing. Children are taught to 'read as writers' as described by Myra Barrs and Valerie Cork in their book *The Reader in the Writer* (Centre For Literacy in Primary Education). Once children have been immersed in these fiction genres and their characters, they will be in a position to use wonderful books as models for their own writing. Children write better in a genre that they have been imaginatively

involved with over a period of time. It is for this reason that many activities in this book help children to understand about writing through the use of good quality texts within genres. As we stressed in the book's introduction, it is important to remember that older children can learn much from picture books. They are some of the most intellectually stimulating books available for children of all ages.

The following is just a small sample of the many terrific books with a huge variety of different characters for all children to enjoy.

Fantasy and spooky
- The **Harry Potter** books – JK Rowling (Bloomsbury)
- *His Dark Materials* trilogy – Philip Pullman (Scholastic)
- *Coraline* – Neil Gaiman (Bloomsbury)
- *The Demon Headmaster* series – Gillian Cross (Puffin)

Historical
- *Witch Child* – Celia Rees (Bloomsbury)
- *Smith* – Leon Garfield (Puffin)
- *The Machine Gunners* – Robert Westall (Macmillan)
- *Goodnight Mister Tom* – Michelle Magorian (Puffin)

Animal stories
- *Black Beauty* – Anna Sewell (various publishers)
- *Mrs Frisby and the Rats of NIMH* – Robert C O'Brien (Puffin)
- *Toad Rage* – Morris Gleitzman (Puffin)
- *Watership Down* – Richard Adams (Red Fox)
- *National Velvet* – Enid Bagnold (various publishers)

Character CVs

This activity helps children to explore characters more deeply. It helps them to understand the importance of creating characters with enough complexity to be believable. The kind of CV we write will often depend upon the job we are applying for (purpose) and who will be reading it (audience). Writing a CV for a character from a book can be a fun way of really getting to know that character. The children will need to look beyond what the book tells them. By recognising the depth and richness of characters in stories, children see the need to develop the characters they invent.

Literature links

Roald Dahl's *Matilda* (Puffin) has rich characterisation. The CVs of Matilda's father or of the headmistress at her school would be interesting. The grandmother in Dahl's *George's Marvellous Medicine* (Puffin) would also stimulate an unusual and funny CV. Also useful are Gillian Cross's *The Demon Headmaster* (Puffin) and JK Rowling's *Harry Potter and the Philosopher's Stone* (Bloomsbury). The characters in the Stories to Tell could also be used, for example Joseph in 'The Call of the Sea' (page 88) and the Jester in 'The Jester and the King' (page 82).

What to do

① Provide the children with a CV framework and explain the purpose of a CV.

② Explain to the children that you are going to write a CV for a character they know, as he or she is applying for a job. You could use a character from the class novel or perhaps the Jester in 'The Jester and the King' (page 82). What kind of past experiences would this character have to write about? Go through the sections on the CV template and help the children to imagine (or recall) his or her address, schools attended and qualifications gained, employment history, any societies belonged to, other skills and interests and so on.

③ Model the writing process. This will essentially involve telling the story of the character's life. For example, *He went to school at X and having gained language and acrobatic and gymnastic qualifications, got his first job as an apprentice jester in Y... After his apprenticeship, he got his first full-time jesting job with Prince A in Z...*

④ Invite the children to work either in pairs or individually to create a CV like this for their character. Allow the children to adapt and edit the CV on a word-processing package. At this stage the children are writing a CV for a character from a story they have been listening to and have enjoyed hearing about. This will encourage them to think deeply about the characters and will influence the construction of characters in their own stories later on.

Moving on

● Before writing their own story, ask the children to write a CV for each of the two main characters in their story. This will assist them in enriching the characterisation in the story they are writing and will form an important part of the planning process and will help to bring their character to life.

Overheard conversations

The drama convention used in this activity is a valuable tool for reflecting on significant characters in a story and for tapping into those characters' perspectives and views about each other. Characters often talk about each other in stories, and reveal strong attitudes. Conversations about characters are likely even if they are not recorded in the text, so it is possible to improvise them and build up knowledge about characters and the relationships they have. This is also a useful shared reading activity that can lead to writing. In essence, this is a form of role-play, but with the added knowledge that the conversation is overheard and was therefore secret or intended to have at least a degree of privacy in the context of the story.

What to do

1 Read up to your chosen moment, and suggest that one of the characters overheard a conversation, or that if they had been near enough this is what they might have heard. Build up the fictional frame by adding details in the voice of a storyteller. For example, using *Bad Girls*:

That night, just as Mandy was dropping off to sleep she heard her mother's strident tones from the landing, 'I don't like her, she's a bad influence you know.' Mandy leaned forward in the darkness to peer onto the landing where her parents stood. Now she would find out what they really thought. She listened intently.

Literature links

Tension or difficulty of some kind needs to be present to trigger conversations that are important or that reveal insights about a character. For example, in *Granny the Pag* by Nina Bawden (Puffin), Catriona may hear gossip or conversation about her granny, who is an unusual character to say the least. In *The Wreck of the Zanzibar* by Michael Morpurgo (Egmont), Laura may overhear her parents discussing her brother Billy's departure on the ship. How do they feel? Do they blame each other? How do their views affect Laura's perspective? In *Goodnight Mister Tom* by Michelle Magorian (Puffin), the young Londoner may accidentally overhear local women in the post office talking about Mr Tom and voicing their concerns about him looking after such a young evacuee. In *Bad Girls* by Jacqueline Wilson (Yearling), Mandy's parents are no doubt concerned about the potential influence of the adolescent Tanya on their young and impressionable daughter. In effect you need to select a moment in a known text when one character may overhear a revealing conversation of some kind.

BAD GIRLS
Jacqueline Wilson
FROM THE AWARD-WINNING AUTHOR OF DOUBLE ACT

© Derek Cooknell

④ Having shared brief snippets from perhaps six or seven groups, discuss what knowledge about the characters has been revealed. Then, focusing on one character, record on the flipchart some of the phrases and attitudes that the groups came up with, as evidenced in the character's words and views towards herself and other characters, and other characters' revelations about her.

② Invite the children in pairs to create the imagined overheard conversation. To work in threes, create the presence of an additional character, for example a grandmother or friend who could have been visiting. Allow time for the children to generate ideas and work through these conversations in their small groups.

⑤ Either as a class in shared writing, or in pairs, work to write a piece of narrative that recounts this overheard conversation.

③ Invite the groups to prepare brief snippets from these conversations for sharing. Suggest they select one or two key pieces of dialogue or narrative that reveal attitudes, and practise these so that if you come to their group they are ready to share this. You are seeking to avoid simple re-enactments of the possible conversations, helping the children to identify the most relevant and meaningful exchanges rather than their first, perhaps stereotypical, ideas. Prompt the children to role-play by voicing the story from the narrator's perspective. For example:

⑥ Encourage the class to read passages of these to their response partners. Their challenge is to discuss how successfully the characters and their relationships have been conveyed through the words, speech verbs and adverbs, intonation, manner and gestures described in the passage.

Moving on

● Extend the role-play and generate ways in which the conversation might come to an end. For example, is Mandy discovered? How do her parents react? Does she toss and turn that night and perhaps wake in the morning to confront her parents? This will shift the focus from characterisation to the moves of the characters within the narrative, but will effectively build upon the ideas generated.

As Mandy slipped into the kitchen to get a drink, she heard her grandmother exclaim, 'Well why don't you stop her from meeting Tanya? Ban her from this friendship, take her on holiday, do something, for goodness' sake!' Mandy missed her mother's reply as the cat flap squeaked behind her, but this is what she heard then…

● List the ideas and insights gained and through discussion seek to divide them into fact and opinion, giving evidence from the improvised oral story or the actual written text.

Conscience alley

© Derek Cooknell

The purpose of this activity is to investigate one character's conscience at a moment of major conflict or a critical decision in the text. The conscience alley technique highlights the complexity of the decision to be taken and reveals the contradictory and challenging thoughts and feelings of the character at this moment. This drama convention can also indicate their relationship with other characters and suggest their perception of the situation. It is an excellent shared reading activity to expand understanding of the character, and it can also lead easily into shared writing that is discursive and weighs up the balance of a situation, the pros and cons of making a certain decision.

Literature links

In fiction, the main characters are frequently faced with momentous decisions. Conscience alleys seek to explore characters' perspectives and concerns at these moments, so almost any book can be employed for this activity. For example, in *Kensuke's Kingdom* by Michael Morpurgo (Egmont), what are the conflicting views in Michael's head when a rescue boat comes into view? He may be able to leave the island, but will also be leaving Kensuke behind. In *Since Dad Left* by Caroline Binch (Frances Lincoln), how does Sid feel when his mother comes to pick him up after his weekend with Dad? In *Children of Winter* by Berlie Doherty (Mammoth), Catherine's mother comes to watch her three children fending for themselves in a barn outside the village of Eyam where she is obliged to dwell because her mother-in-law is dying of the plague. In *Shadow Spinner* by Susan Fletcher (Bloomsbury), Marjan has to decide whether to return to the harem, try to save Shahrazad and confront the Sultan or whether to escape, to put her own safety first and save her own skin. The struggle in her conscience can be created at this moment as she reflects in the darkness of Abu Moslem's house and her conflicting views, loyalties and hopes can be expressed through the conscience alley. In *Angus Rides the Goods Train* by Alan Durant (Corgi), Angus has to decide whether to accept the injustice he sees or take action. It may be a split second decision, but no doubt many thoughts flash through his mind. A conscience alley seeks to evoke these thoughts.

What to do

1. Select a moment in your chosen story when a main character has to face a difficult situation and make a critical decision. Read up to this moment, sharing the author's perspective on the dilemma.

2. Invite the children to create two lines facing one another, rather in the manner of country dancing! Explain to the class that this is going to help them get inside the head and conscience of the character to see how he or she feels at this moment.

3. Recap the situation in the story and give the children time to discuss with someone next to them in their line what the character might be thinking and feeling. This should generate a variety of ideas.

4. Invite one child, in role as the character (or take on the role yourself), and explain that in a moment, this person will need to walk down the conscience alley and listen to their conflicting thoughts voiced aloud before making a decision. For example, in *Children of Winter,* should Catherine's mother just go and hug her son, or take food and clothes to her starving children, all of whom need their mother's love. The child, in role as the character, will need to listen to 'her' thoughts and feelings spoken aloud and make up her mind based on what she has heard.

5. Re-read the passage from the story to frame the conscience alley and provide the immediate narrative context.

6. Encourage the child in role to walk slowly down the alley, listening to each of the children's first person narrative perspectives in turn. For example, in *Children of Winter*, the mother may be saying to herself:

- They need me, I must go to them.
- What if the plague is carried in the air?
- I have eggs, the children will die without food. I must go.
- I've touched the eggs, and my children may catch the plague from them and die.
- My Ben will be so happy when he sees me.

Encourage the children to speak loudly enough for the rest of the class to hear.

7. When the child has reached the end of the alley, ask him or her, based upon what they have heard, what the decision would be and why. Often, children will be able to identify one or two views that tipped the balance one way or the other.

8. List the different views and thoughts and categorise these as for or against the mother going to her children. You are thus creating a list of pros and cons that can be used as a basis for diary or letter writing. Such writing will highlight the range of persuasive/discursive arguments that shaped the decision, so the reader gains insight into the character's motivation, attitudes and thinking.

9. Read on in the text to share the decision the mother makes or simply inhabit this moment and afterwards share the choice that the author made for the character.

Moving on

- You could invite the children to take sides and suggest that each half of the alley represents one side of the argument, for and against a particular decision. This can create an imbalanced alley, but will reflect the children's perspectives more explicitly.

- You might undertake the activity by letting the children stand anywhere in the room, rather than in lines, and the child in role walks around listening to the views offered. This effectively reflects the confused and often contradictory state of mind of the character at this moment in the story.

Role on the wall

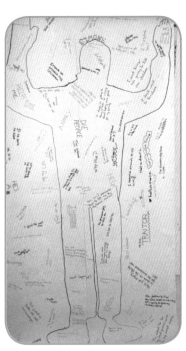

A role on the wall is, in essence, the body shape of a character. Other characters' perspectives of the figure are recorded outside the outline, while the character's own views and feelings are noted inside. The purpose of the activity is to develop insight into a character, both from the perspective of other characters and from his or her own sense of self. It is useful to document the development of and changes to a character during a long novel and can be revealing to identify the views of others about this individual at various points in the tale. A large role on the wall outline can be displayed just before beginning to read a novel and added to throughout the study of the book or replicated for additional moments. It can contribute to the growing body of knowledge about the character.

Literature links

Any text can be used for this activity, but the moments to create or add to a role in the wall need to carefully selected. In a novel, it is useful to identify a single or series of challenging or climatic moments, or a series of roles on the wall can be developed at several significant points in the story. For example, in *Harry Potter and the Philosopher's Stone* by JK Rowling (Bloomsbury), an early role on the wall could reflect Uncle Vernon, Aunt Petunia and Dudley's views about Harry. Later in the text, Hermione's, Ron's, Draco Malfoy's and Hagrid's perspectives could be recorded, while Professor Dumbledore's, Professor Snape's and Voldemort's views could be recorded at a crucial closing event. Other examples include a role on the wall for Jim in *Street Child* by Berlie Doherty (Lions), Tom in *Tom's Midnight Garden* by Philippa Pearce (Puffin), for Leje in 'The Weaving of a Dream' (page 84) or for Hattie in *The Great Elephant Chase* by Gillian Cross (OUP).

What to do

❶ Select a character from your current class novel or the next story you intend to read, and identify a moment of particular interest early in the narrative. Read up to that moment or the chapter before and the immediate framing passages. For example, in *Street Child* by Berlie Doherty, Jim Jarvis could be the role on the wall and his views could be recorded when he first arrives at the workhouse.

❷ With a fat felt-tipped pen, draw around a child lying on a long sheet of paper or roll of lining paper. This will give the outline for the role on the wall.

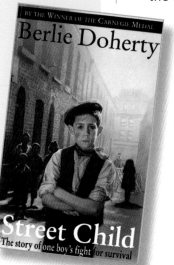

Timeline of events from *Street Child*

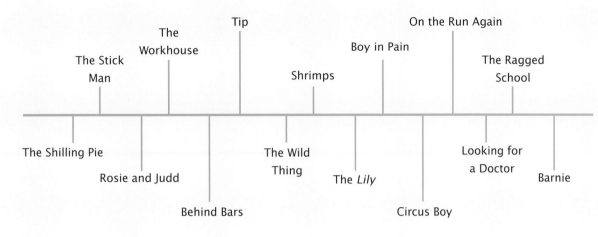

③ Remind the class of the chosen situation in the story, and perhaps re-read a short passage, for example, that which describes Jim's initial loneliness and fear following his separation from his sisters.

④ Ask the children to gather around the role on the wall, which might be entitled 'Jim Jarvis arrives at the workhouse', and ask them to record the character's thoughts and feelings at this moment by writing them inside the body shape. At the end of chapter 5 in *Street Child*, Jim realises that his mother is dead and he is condemned to a life in the workhouse. How does he feel? What is he thinking? Ask the children to read several of their examples out loud.

⑤ Compose a paragraph of interior monologue in the style of the book, using some of the material from the role on the wall. Show the children how they might integrate their ideas into a paragraph.

⑥ Read another situation from the novel where another character's view of your chosen character is given, for example, the paragraph in *Street Child* in which Jim makes a friend and experiences school with Mr Barrack.

⑦ Invite the class to record another character's perspective (for example, Tip or Mr Barrack's views of Jim) around the outside of the role on the wall figure.

⑧ As a class, individually or in pairs, the children could compose another imagined paragraph for the story, for example in which Mr Barrack tells another character about Jim, using some of the ideas, phrases and raw material from the role on the wall.

Moving on

● Display this role on the wall as part of a simple timeline that encompasses chapter titles. Then undertake two further roles on the wall in the context of your chosen novel. Using *Street Child* as an example, you could record Jim's temporary happiness when he is hiding at Rosie's and making friends with Shrimps. Also examine his feelings when he is working for Grimy Nick, particularly when he tries to escape, or when he believes he has killed Nick and Snipe, or when Shrimps dies. These roles on the wall can be displayed on the timeline.

● Track the development of the main character through the roles on the wall, identifying through his words and phrases and others', how, for example, Jim gains confidence, physical strength, and develops cunning and determination through his ordeals.

Forum theatre

This activity enables children to consider characters' actions, reactions and relationships and discuss their likely behaviour and motives, justifying their point of view with reference to the text. The activity takes the form of an improvisation performed by a few children in role as characters from the text, which is watched by the rest of the class in the theatre forum of the classroom. During the drama action, 'time outs' are taken to enable the class to offer advice and suggestions to the children in role. Then the scene is revisited and re-shaped in response to the advice given.

What to do

❶ Read up to your chosen extract. For example, in *The Angel of Nitshill Road* by Anne Fine, at the end of chapter 1, Mark, Marigold and Penny summon up the courage to speak to Mr Fairway about the bullying they are enduring. You may need to invent a reasonable fictional scenario around the focus issues in the text, or give the children the context of the extract and some background about the particular scene.

❷ Ask the children to improvise the scene in groups of four. Let them have some time to discuss the options, for example where the scene will take place, who will be there and so on. For example, in *The Angel of Nitshill Road,* was a casual opportunity seized by the children or did they visit Mr Fairway in the staff room? Gauge the likely formality of the characters' meeting.

❸ Observe the groups as they improvise, then invite one group to share their improvisation as a piece of forum theatre in the classroom. Create a space for them to perform in, and arrange the rest of the class in seated positions so they can see. You do not need the 'best' group, just a group of children who are prepared to share, listen to and act on advice that may be offered.

❹ Watch this improvisation as a class.

Literature links

Almost any text can be used for forum theatre, but select a tense and/or significant moment in a story that will reveal the nature of various characters and their reactions to other characters at this potentially difficult moment. In *The Diary of Anne Frank* there are several challenging situations that could be used, such as improvisations at the meal table the night the burglars visit the warehouse below. Other possible examples include moments in *No Turning Back* by Beverley Naidoo (Puffin), *Double Act* by Jacqueline Wilson (Yearling) or

The Angel of Nitshill Road by Anne Fine (Egmont). The activity will work best if the children already have a fairly good knowledge of the main characters involved in the scene to be presented.

⑤ At a reasonably early point in the drama scene, intervene and, divide the audience into advice groups. Ask each actor to join one of the groups. The groups need to suggest alternative ways of behaving for the characters, explaining their reasons and possibly offering suggestions for dialogue as well. For example, *I don't think Marigold would shout at Mr Fairway. She may be angry inside but she's not confident enough to shout – she would probably whisper, 'Please listen to us we're fed up and afraid'.*

⑥ If the children find this commentary too challenging, you may wish to model it first, offering your constructive ideas with regard to one character in the improvisation. In fact, it may be helpful for you or the classroom assistant to take part in the improvisation as well, so that the children initially comment upon your in-role behaviour, justifying the reasons for their comments by making reference to the text.

⑦ Encourage the actors to take the advice offered. Restart the improvisation with this in mind and allow the drama to develop a little further this time.

⑧ Intervene once again and discuss as a class whether the behaviour now shown by the characters is more or less appropriate than the earlier example. Why? What feelings are revealed (or hidden)?

⑨ You can continue in this manner for as long as seems useful, with the class shaping the theatre they are watching and focusing on the likely speech, behaviour and motives of the key characters at this moment in their story.

© Derek Cooknell

Moving on

● As a class or individually, write up a your scene either as a script, or as a passage as it would appear in the story. The script could encompass the actions and moves of the key characters as depicted in the improvisation. The scene as it appears in the story could be read and compared with the script or class-produced passage.

● The forum theatre can also be performed in the middle of a class circle, with the audience being invited to clap and intervene when they perceive a character is acting in an unlikely or inappropriate manner and they have alternative suggestions to make which they can support with reference to the text.

● Suggest to the children that a week later another incident happens in the same setting and the main characters are all once again involved. Allow them to suggest ideas in groups for what the incident might be, then invite them to write it as part of the story, making use of the insights they gained about the characters in the forum theatre.

Changing characters

© Lauren Child

This is a simple activity that asks children to substitute a character from a well-known tale for another character that the children have chosen themselves. This character may be another well-known character from a different story, perhaps from a film rather than a book, or it may be a character that a child has created. The children need to adapt the details of the swapped character to fit the context of his or her new story. In addition, the other characters who inhabit this world will also need to be altered to deal with this change. In order to do this, the children must know both the story and the character really well so they can bond these 'strange bedfellows' together. The activity can be a challenge, but a great deal of fun.

Literature links

Clarice Bean from the various Clarice Bean novels by Lauren Child, is a lovely character with lots of potential to send on her travels to another story. You might want to use characters from films, particularly animation, for example Sid the Sloth from *Ice Age* or Buzz Lightyear from the *Toy Story* films. This converts the medium of the story and the characters from film, to book. Consider, for example, how Buzz Lightyear might react to replacing Jack in 'Jack and the Beanstalk'. Could Clarice Bean survive replacing Cinderella? The possibilities are mind-boggling and full of potential, and

What to do

❶ As a shared activity, ask the children to brainstorm their favourite characters from film, television, books and comics. List these down the left-hand side of the flipchart or on an OHT. The children will have no trouble thinking of their favourites, particularly when they can choose from different media. Then brainstorm some famous and favourite stories all of the children know. Write these on the right-hand side of the paper.

❷ Now have some fun linking characters to stories, speculating about who

© Lauren Child

children will enjoy disrupting the chemistry of many familiar stories by injecting unexpected characters into them. This activity works particularly well as the culmination of a unit of work on traditional stories and would make entertaining reading for all the class if the resulting stories with their new characters are put into the class reading library alongside the more traditional versions.

© Derek Cooknell

retelling, with the imported characters, will be made into a book for the reading area.

⑤ Invite the children to plan their stories in the form of a story-map. Using large sheets of paper, explain that they will need to note down the key moments from the story, then annotate each of these in relation to the new character. This 'map' could be in the form of simple labelled diagrams or straight text. Encourage them to note if any key events no longer happen and what new events might occur instead.

⑥ Once they are happy with their story maps, the children can draft their stories and work towards a final publication for the class library. Encourage them to illustrate them with drawings, paintings or photographs. You may want to make this activity the closing one to a unit of work on a particular kind of text, so you may well decide to make the end result as lavish as your resources can provide.

they could substitute and what exactly might happen to the character and to the story. You could assist the children in thinking of some of the problems the change may create. For example, how would a modern character like Clarice Bean cope in 'Snow White', without being able to watch television or use the telephone, which had yet to be invented?

③ As a class, choose one character and one story. Run through the story's narrative, thinking about each of the key events and how the new character would respond in those situations. Consider the other characters that would be met. How would the interaction develop? Would this change the story? What new events might occur as a result of the new character's intervention?

④ Next ask the children to work in pairs on a story with a new character. Advise them that this can be a character of their own invention, or one of their favourites from the flipchart. Tell the children that this

Moving on

● As an alternative, invite the children to substitute themselves for the key protagonists in the stories. With this activity they can draw on their knowledge of their own character and how they would react to these new circumstances.

● Ask the children to learn their new stories for an oral performance. These may well include some comedy moments, so in the script writing or preparation, help the children use dialogue and stage directions to maximise the effect of comedy timing, for example.

The character in the pictures

In this activity, children focus on characterisation through examination of illustrations. The children study different images that accompany a variety of retellings of a traditional tale. The children will be asked a number of questions about the character as depicted by the images. Different retellings across history depict Little Red Riding Hood, for example, in different ways and she is a good character to choose. In some stories, she is the innocent, tricked by the wolf to walk away from the safe path in the wood; in others, she is a modern, feisty heroine, prepared to go to any lengths to stop the wolf having his way. In feminist retellings, Red Riding Hood and Granny kill the wolf with no help from men! The children can be invited to retell the tale as told from a chosen character's point of view, supported by the way the character is depicted in the illustration they choose to use.

What to do

❶ Show the children the collection of illustrations of the same character by different artists. If it is not practical to show them all together, discuss them one at a time. Ask, for example:

Literature links

This activity works particularly well during a unit of work on traditional tales. It explores traditional tales from a slightly unusual and engaging angle. You will need to choose a particular tale of which you know there are multiple versions available. The tale will need to have a strong, clearly defined main character or characters, for example Little Red Riding Hood, Cinderella, the Three Little Pigs or Snow White. You will need to know that the books have good examples of images depicting the characters at different parts of the story.

© Chris Fisher

Little Head Riding Pudd

Catherine Orenstein's fascinating book *Little Red Riding Hood Uncloaked* (Basic Books) shows a number of illustrations depicting the heroine. In *The Juniper Tree and Other Tales from Grimm* edited by Lore Segal (Bodley Head), Maurice Sendak's representations of the famous fairy story characters are particularly intriguing. Roald Dahl's *Revolting Rhymes* (Puffin) depicts favourite characters in very different and amusing ways.

- Can you say which part of the tale the picture illustrates?
- What has happened directly before and directly after the event in the image?
- Does the picture give any clue as to how the tale is told in this version? Will it be scary, funny, or dull?
- How would you describe the character as he or she is shown in this image?
- What do you think will happen at the end of this version of the tale? Why?

It may not be appropriate to ask all of the questions about each picture. You could encourage the children to order the pictures by age. Is there anything about the images that gives clues to how when they were created? Are any images particularly modern or particularly old fashioned?

② Next, ask pairs of children to choose one version of the character from your discussions to build their own retelling around. Ask them to discuss how their version of this tale should be retold according to how the scene, and in particular the character, is depicted in the image they have chosen. Invite the partners to examine their version of the character closely. What is significant about the way he or she has been depicted? What is going on around him or her, if anything? How do they think they can use the illustration to build their own retelling of the tale?

③ Encourage the children to use their discussion to draw a simple story map that provides the key elements of the tale. This will help them see the way the story will go. If you have found some good examples, the children should be able to write some very different versions of the same story.

④ Organise the class so that the pairs of children can tell their version of the story to another group, emphasising the character traits of the main protagonist as depicted in the original illustration.

⑤ The pair can then write their own versions of the story based on the illustration they have chosen. The oral retelling will have helped them to flesh this out. Once the stories have been written, make sure all the children can have access to them, perhaps in the classroom library.

Moving on

- Ask the children to draw their own illustration of a character from another traditional tale that indicates the way they would want the character to be depicted in a new retelling. This could then form the basis of a written retelling. Before writing their story, the children could write around their picture the personality traits and significant viewpoints of their character and how he or she will be portrayed. This could take the form of a spider diagram with the illustration placed in the centre.

© Derek Cooknell

Character profiles

This activity examines the story vocabulary used to create strong and identifiable characters and helps to explore the potential for the children to develop this understanding and create a full character profile. The children will be encouraged to 'zoom in' on high-profile characters, enhancing the image already offered. This will enable them to develop a repertoire of their own when creating characters in their story writing. As high quality texts are read and examined, the children will be able to detect how characters are allowed to develop through a story as events impact on their lives.

Literature links

This activity will work well with any story that offers a rich description of characters, particularly those with whom children of this age can identify. The work of David Almond, for example in *Kit's Wilderness* or *Heaven Eyes* (both Hodder & Stoughton) would be good for this purpose as these have strong central characters who experience both emotional and physical challenges. This will engage children who might have different expectations of the stories. Gillian Cross's *Tightrope* (Puffin) or *Fruit and Nutcase* by Jean Ure (Collins) would also help children to follow a complex character through a challenging set of events.

What to do

❶ Select a book that is either already known to the children or that is currently being read with them. Focus on one character, revisiting the text at the point at which he or she is first introduced.

❷ Read this first description from the text and ask the children to note words or phrases that are key to this introduction to the character. It would be useful at this stage, with more experienced readers and writers, to examine language of inference as well as literal references, for example in any texts written in the first person. With less experienced readers, the focus will probably remain on adjectives and adverbs to support their understanding of the characters.

❸ Discuss what is known about the character at this stage of the novel – his or her appearance, interests, how s/he feels and so on, referring to the text to identify key language. In *Fruit and Nutcase*, we know at the beginning that Mandy is sparky and creative, and that her good, if irreverent, relationship with her parents is of great importance to her.

❹ Ask the children to work in pairs to create questions to ask about the character at

© Derek Cooknell

● Using another story that the children know, they could work in small groups or pairs to select a character and develop the descriptions of him or her from the text. This could be done orally at first, with one partner requesting information, for example, *Tell me more about Mandy. Is it true that Tracey can't hurt her?* This would be carried out with the support of brainstorms or notes made, and then retold to other groups. The test of whether or not the character is convincing would be in the power of the language used by the children in this retelling, whether or not further questions still exist in their audience's mind, and whether these questions detract from the power of the story or add to it by, for example, making a character particularly intriguing. With more experienced readers and writers, explore whether or not the more questions the author leaves readers with, the more powerful the characterisation becomes. These new texts could then be further developed in guided writing sessions, particularly focusing on looking for synonyms in descriptive language.

this stage of the novel and list these. In *Fruit and Nutcase*, for example, who is Cat? Does Mandy have any other friends?

⑤ Looking at key passages in the novel, revisit the character as the story unfolds, using the text to answer earlier questions and raise new ones. This part of the activity would work well with the whole class feeding into a discussion. The first passage may need to be identified for the children but they could then contribute to the selection of passages that help in this character focus. They will need to revisit the text for this purpose, which will involve them in personally re-reading passages and identifying some for inclusion in the discussion.

⑥ Discuss how some questions are answered through the novel and how others are left unanswered and possible reasons for this.

⑦ As a whole class, using the shared text and the questions raised, retell parts of the story, developing the characterisation by enhancing the author's presentation with the children's additions.

● To further support children's use of language in characterisation, a known story character could be chosen to be hot-seated. Enrich this by having more than one child role-play the character at different points in the story. In this way, character development and viewpoint could be considered, with children's questions (and answers) reflecting their increased experience of the character, knowledge of the story so far and the need (and ability) to construct a fully rounded picture of the individual.

Emotions graph

This activity encourages children to explore the feelings of a character within a strong narrative and to represent these feelings in the form of a graph. By now, the children will have met a wide variety of characters in a range of settings and will have developed favourites. They will feel empathy with some and not with others, in the way that experienced readers do, and this engagement will work across media and in and out of school. Children can often, at this age, be heard in the playground discussing characters from television soap operas and very popular books, almost as if they existed in their lives. They predict events, analyse characters and stage-manage their affairs and their lives. Drawing on these experiences, and their understanding of characters and character development, will be useful in a classroom context. The children will discuss their views of characters and articulate their feelings, empathy, or lack of interest in them. This will help the children to use descriptive language and to understand how events in a story impact on a character to effect change in attitude and emotions. It will also support them in understanding the ways in which the relationships between characters can be constructed and manipulated to progress the story.

Literature links

This activity will work well with short stories or oral tales, so that in one session, without struggling to remember how the story has developed, children can easily detect the points in the story at which events create change and when the character changes emotional direction. A short but sophisticated story, such as Anthony Browne's *Voices in the Park* or Geraldine McCaughrean's *Beauty and the Beast* (both Picture Corgi) could be used to start children thinking in this way and as a model for other, texts. Alternatively, an oral telling of, for example 'The Call of the Sea' (page 88) or the African tale 'Children of Wax' (you might be able to find a version by Alexander McCall Smith or a film version) would also be appropriate as the children could quickly see how events changed to affect the emotions of main characters.

What to do

❶ Read or tell your chosen story. Discuss its structure, characters, setting and events, giving the children time to respond to the story. You might want to focus at first on particularly memorable, challenging, frightening or sad moments.

❷ Examine more closely the emotions evoked by the story, choosing one character as the focus. For example, in 'The Call of the Sea', explore Joseph's or

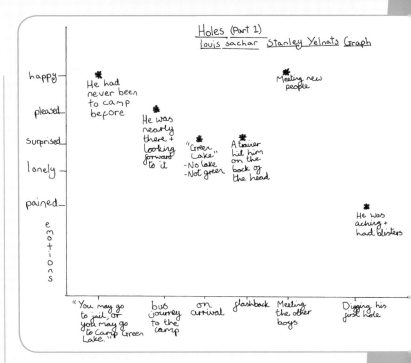

the mermaid's emotions at different points in the story. Enrich the descriptions of the mermaid in a shared writing activity, creating a full picture of her from what we know from the tale.

❸ From this full picture, discuss how, in 'Children of Wax' for example, the sister would be feeling as the eldest of the children, how she views her responsibilities, her life and her frustrations.

❹ Draw the two axes of a line graph on the flipchart. On the horizontal axis, mark points in the story that are significant for this character. For example, at the beginning, when the girl's parents had high expectations at the birth of her younger siblings, then when each day begins, then when each night begins, then at play, until the whole story is briefly plotted. On the vertical axis, make evenly spaced marks to represent the changes in feelings of the character.

❺ Go through the story, inviting the children to plot the changing emotions of the character at each point. Initially, the children could be asked just to mark the graph to show, for example, the sister's anxiety when Ngwabi begins to scratch a hole in the wall. Through discussion, annotations could be included to support their decision so that, where the original graph merely had points or stars marked to determine where anxiety occurred or she was content, as the discussion developed words would appear to help define the moment. This part of the activity will develop the children's use of emotive verbs.

❻ Ask the children to work in pairs or small groups to retell the story from the viewpoint of the character, focusing their descriptions on his or her feelings.

❼ In a guided writing session, help the children to formalise their oral retellings and use the emotions graph to create a

written character sketch that will develop the character from the oral tale, consolidate their use of the language of description and add depth to their characterisations.

Moving on

● This way of working could be extended to include a range of stories. Provide the children with a collection from which to select, in pairs, a story with a suitably developed character. They could then develop individual emotion graphs, each based on a different character from the same story. Further develop this by challenging the children to swap graphs and use them to retell the story from the other character's viewpoint.

● Display an emotion graph that you have created with the class. Read a particularly poignant or powerful part of the story, perhaps just a phrase or short paragraph, and challenge the children to identify where on the graph that section belongs. Alternatively, identify a point on the graph and challenge the children to use the most powerful language at their disposal to retell that section of the story. This could be done as a class or in pairs.

Media interviews

This role-play can be developed into an exercise in writing in a particular genre for a particular audience. Journalistic writing is a demanding form, but there are many good examples to use as models. Use the activity to challenge children to write in this style, while drawing on their knowledge of story characters to help the writing come to life. The children will be getting inside the mind of a character to imagine responses to questions that would not necessarily have been met in the story.

What to do

❶ Agree on a character to focus on in a model. Choose a volunteer to be interviewed in role, or model the interview with a classroom assistant. The interviewer should ask clear but open-ended questions. The interviewee should give answers appropriate, interesting and suitable for further questioning. The interview should flow like a less formal conversation.

❷ Quickly brainstorm what the children might want to ask the characters, based on the story. Look for examples that will generate interesting answers. Suggest that these form a basic list of questions for the children's paired interviews.

❸ Ask the children in pairs to decide which character from the story they intend to interview and to organise themselves into reporter and interviewee, then role-play the conversation. Go around the pairs, looking out for leading questions and answers that show understanding of the character.

❺ Share some of the questions and responses. Revisit the story and ask the children if their understanding of the characters has changed. Have they noticed different viewpoints? Do they see different meanings in the story?

Literature links

Find stories with strong characters. Your current class book may be suitable, or try *The Amazing Bible Storybook* by Georgie Adams (Orion). For fantasy stories, use Terry Pratchett's *Only You Can Save Mankind (Corgi)*. Paul Jennings's *The Gizmo (Puffin)* is a hilarious tale, or you could use one of the Stories to Tell from this book. It would be useful to share some interviews from news/current affairs/magazine programmes or chat shows.

Moving on

● In shared writing, compose an interview article drawing on the role-play. This could lead to the interview pairs composing their own article, which could include the children's illustrations of the characters interviewed and be desktop published. They would make a wonderful display alongside genuine magazine articles to highlight the features of this kind of writing.

Chapter Three

Story Settings

Our memories of favourite stories from childhood cannot be separated from the worlds in which they are set: the fantasy palaces, forests and cottages of fairy tales, or the bedrooms, gardens, treetops, dens or parks of modern stories. Readers' memories of places in stories are not those of merely an onlooker. They have a sense of inhabiting those settings alongside the characters, of feeling the fear inside the wild woods or smelling the familiar air of classrooms and playgrounds.

Locating these memories for young writers is important as they begin the challenge of creating landscapes for their characters and readers to inhabit. Encouraging children to consider what they can see, hear, smell and touch will help them to construct complete settings. Gathering such impressions and seeing with their 'mind's eye' will help young writers to become more and more observant as they collect ideas for their stories from home, school, their streets and their lives.

The challenge of encouraging children to create, explore and shape settings for stories can be met in a variety of motivating ways in the classroom. To emphasise the significance of a story's context, it will be necessary to use quality texts from various media to create opportunities for discussion, exploration and inspiration. Immersion in the work of skilful storytellers and illustrators in picture fiction, short stories and novels will help children to identify, compare and contrast familiar, far away and fantastic settings. Children's fascination for film and television can also be used to help them become engaged in constructing scenes in which to set their stories.

Children need to be consistently supported by the work of experienced story makers as they develop understanding of how the place in which a narrative is set influences the characters and the nature of the story. Such evaluative and critical work will help children to understand the craft used by authors and illustrators in creating worlds in which to set characters and events.

Out of school, children at this age are making connections and deconstructing complex texts in subtle ways and at different levels. Firstly, visual images have become extremely significant in children's lives generally. They are used to the world of advertisements, for example, where images are used to tantalise, excite and persuade. They also grow accustomed in their out-of-school lives to using sophisticated skills of reading to interpret complex and often humorous texts that portray certain lifestyles, sell products or simply entertain, as in comics and magazines. Authors often use experiences and landscapes from their own lives to influence the settings of their stories; so children of this age should also be persuaded to draw on these and to match their memories and visual experiences of home, school, television and other media to their

fast developing, active written vocabulary. Secondly, children are often exposed to the juxtaposition of ideas. For example, an advertisement may set a child in a grown up world, or put a man in a city suit in a desert in order to make a particular marketing point. Superheroes or cartoon characters may be found unexpectedly in different world contexts on television or in film. In this way, children learn to view a place through the eyes of the character, perhaps informed by their own experience. Connections can be made from this to the creation of journey stories, where characters find themselves encountering different landscapes on their journey towards a resolution.

Thirdly, from the early years of their lives, children have learned the skills of subversion. It is a major feature of their lives, their play, their language and their humour. This ability to turn things around, to add a twist, to play with language, to create a topsy-turvy approach to life and language, is second nature to most children, who will often instinctively look for the unusual or the distorted view rather than a straightforward method or outcome. Stories where humour like this is at least partly created by the setting can be found in the work of Anthony Browne, through his deceptively simple picture books that often contain sophisticated themes and humour.

© Photodisc, Inc.

These three areas of expertise – a sophisticated visual experience, juxtaposition and sense of the unusual, and subversion – combine to enable the construction of a creative, playful and visual sense of story setting. Children at this stage are ready to appreciate the work, for example, of Philip Pullman in the *His Dark Materials* trilogy as he creates other worlds and cleverly juxtaposes ideas, places, characters and time. Such encounters, through discussion, retelling, examination and exploration, will lead children to the possibility of testing techniques like these in their own writing.

In the classroom it is important to capitalise on these skills to help children create unique stories that may incorporate patterns and models from traditional and contemporary tales, but also contain the influence of the children's own experiences. For example, setting a traditional tale in modern times (or vice versa), would engage the children in literary problem-solving at a range of different levels. Oral work is essential as children come to understand the tale and redevelop it in a place of their own. This would involve classroom practices of collaboration, drama techniques and debate. Children would need to draw on the existing literary text and other comparable examples to support their understanding of how time and place influences the narrative. Examining story openings in particular would be a useful beginning to help them build their own story set.

The use of film would be appropriate for children at this stage, particularly if the film has been constructed from a novel. For example, *Goodnight Mister Tom* by Michelle Magorian could be carefully examined for its construction of visual images from the original written text. The children would need to explore the language used to create a sense of the time in history and the place in the novel before examining how this text had been transposed into a visual version. Using film in this way would not only take children further inside the story being studied but would also begin to provide some insight into how the use of this media effects the reconstruction of the text. Changes in sequences of events, different emphases in the narrative and characters, as well as choices and forms of settings, could form part of children's work on media. Children of all ages will be highly motivated to work with film and their excitement often grows as they begin to uncover the 'secrets' of film makers and learn to try out ideas for themselves.

These early trials would probably take the form of storyboarding, although exploring potential settings inside and around their school could also be beneficial to their understanding of how landscapes or settings impact on stories.

It will be useful for you and the children to become familiar with a variety of stories that are noticeable for their particular settings. Books that will help children to understand and categorise settings might be found under these headings:

The sea
- **Sea-Cat and Dragon King** – Angela Carter (Bloomsbury)
- **Daughter of the Sea** – Berlie Doherty (Puffin)
- **The Big Big Sea** – Martin Waddell (Walker Books)
- **The Wreck of the Zanzibar** – Michael Morpurgo (Egmont)

School
- **The Demon Headmaster** – Gillian Cross (Puffin)
- **The Turbulent Term of Tyke Tiler** – Gene Kemp (Collins)
- **How to Write Really Badly** – Anne Fine (Egmont)
- **Bill's New Frock** – Anne Fine (Egmont)

Towns
- **Fair's Fair** (Hodder & Stoughton) and **Smith** (Puffin) – Leon Garfield
- **The Day of Ahmed's Secret** – Florence Parry Heide and Judith Heide Gilliland (Puffin)
- **Wolf** – Gillian Cross (Puffin)
- **Snow White in New York** – Fiona French (OUP)

The countryside
- **Farm Boy** – Michael Morpurgo (HarperCollins)
- **The Railway Children** – E Nesbit (various publishers)
- **Goodnight Mister Tom** – Michelle Magorian (Puffin)
- **The Sheep-Pig** – Dick King-Smith (Puffin)
- **Charlotte's Web** – EB White (Puffin).

Personal replacement

This activity invites children to enter a fantasy world of their choice. By imagining this new world the children will generate a description of a place very different from the one they are used to. Writing settings well requires authors to generate ideas imaginatively. In the same way that the reader must 'see' the places that authors write about, the author has to do this while composing. Drama and role-play can help children do this. By the time they have reached nine, children are masters

Literature links

A unit of work on fantasy writing fits well with this activity, but it would also work well with almost any kind of setting you may be encouraging the children to write. If the class are looking at fantasy stories, there are many wonderful books to choose from. Try *Artemis Fowl* by Eoin Colfer (Puffin) or Susan Cooper's *The Dark is Rising* (Puffin) or, of course, *The Lord of the Rings* by JRR Tolkien (HarperCollins). Philip Pullman's *Northern Lights* (Scholastic) is also excellent. Working with these kinds of books immerses the children in the fantasy worlds that are created by the authors and establishes a model of this kind of writing. The children's engagement with these texts will have been intellectual as the stories invite children to picture the settings described and explored. They will have understood what the impact of these books is and this will influence their own writing immensely.

of play, imagining new worlds and new situations for their games to take place in. Creating stories can be seen as a form of play that also needs this kind of experience. Asking children to imagine in this way should enable them to enrich their writing by drawing on their vibrant minds to write believable and evocative settings.

What to do

1 Although children are experts in this kind of imaginative play, they may feel a little self-conscious if not experienced in it as schoolwork. The best way to encourage involvement is to remember that this drama does not require any performance. The experience of being in role in itself is what we are after.

2 Create some space in the classroom so the children can move around a little. Explain to them that they are about to enter one of the fantasy worlds they have been reading about. You could suggest that

The scorching sun is high in the sky. The heat is like a weight on my shoulders. A whipping breeze blows sand around my feet and dust into my face. I can just hear a swinging sign groaning in the dusty little town.

they will be stepping through a hole cut by the Subtle Knife (from Philip Pullman's *His Dark Materials)* to discover this new world. Explain that you are the expedition leader and they must follow your instructions. Tell them that the world may be dangerous, in terms of climate and the creatures that may live there.

③ Invite the children to pretend to pack their expedition rucksacks. They could check in pairs that everyone has what they think will be needed (sleeping bags, weapons, food, drink and so on).

④ Cut the hole between the worlds and step through it, followed by the children. The children will follow you through in a line. You could keep the hole open and help them through, signalling for them to stay quiet and directing them to where they should stand in this world (the classroom).

⑤ When the children are all through, ask one or two of them to tell you the first thing they can see. Ask for more description if necessary. You may wish to model the imaginative process by saying what you can see and then asking the children. Already they will be actively engaged in the imaginative process of composition, drawing on their own vocabulary to describe a fantasy setting.

⑥ Ask the children to write down what they can see, hear, smell and feel. They are all in the same world together and each description will link to another. The children's experiences will differ, but one fantasy world is constructed. Encourage the children to use descriptive words that give a sense of atmosphere and indicate how they are feeling in this strange new world. The children need to draw on their senses – is it quiet and still, or is a fierce wind blowing? Is the sun shining and how high in the sky is it? Are there mountains, or is this a deserted town? What are the houses like? Do they feel safe, or is there something that they find disturbing?

© Derek Cooknell

⑦ Tell the children their objective on the expedition is to collect four specimens to bring back to the classroom. This will depend upon the environment you have constructed together. It may be rock samples, clothing, plant life or food. Ask them to write down what they have found.

⑧ Bring the children back into the classroom, and share descriptions of some of the finds.

⑧ In shared writing, weave some of the children's ideas into a description of a fantasy world. Then ask the children to work individually on drafting their own setting for a story. The objects they have collected will inform this.

Page 53

Moving on

● Introduce a new element into the drama action. For example, you or a teaching assistant could go into role as a native of this fantasy world. You might invite the visiting children to a feast to celebrate their arrival. In role, work with the children to fix a menu of foods they might enjoy. Or perhaps they will need to speak to the leader of this world and convince him or her that they really do come in peace and are not there to exploit their natural resources.

Special places

This activity helps children to build their descriptive language, which will enhance their settings. Reminding the children of texts they know well and those they are currently reading, and drawing their attention to cleverly chosen words, phrases and paragraphs that support the construction of descriptive narratives, will enhance their writing. They will also be supported in considering how texts can be rooted in the writer's experiences of places and helped to write their own examples of descriptive language. This activity will move between shared writing activities, paired independent work and guided writing in order to provide an initial model, a collaborative activity and an opportunity to redraft and refine their writing. The children will be asked to create a sense of atmosphere and to work collaboratively on descriptive language to define their special places.

What to do

❶ Begin by reading a section from a story, or a whole story, that describes setting effectively. Ask for responses to the use of language to create a sense of the setting. Brainstorm some of the descriptive terms used and write them on the flipchart.

❷ Tell the children about a special place in your life, perhaps somewhere that holds exciting memories or emotional connections for you, or a place shared with someone special in your life (such as a holiday destination, grandma's garden, your house). Explain why this is special, using language that reflects what can be seen, heard and felt. Emphasise detail.

❸ Create a quiet and special atmosphere in the classroom. Ask the children to close their eyes and see themselves in a space that is special to them. Encourage them to remember it with all their senses. You

Literature links

Stories offering very expressive language and evocative language in descriptions of settings will act as a model for the children's own writing. For example, in *Daughter of the Sea* by Berlie Doherty (Puffin), very brief but very powerful descriptions are used to evoke a sense of place: *My tale is of the sea. It takes place in the far north, where ice has broken land into jagged rocks, and where black and fierce tides wash the shores.* Other books suitable both for this age range and for the study of setting could include *The Wreck of the Zanzibar* (Egmont) and *Farm Boy* (HarperCollins) by Michael Morpurgo or *Fair's Fair* by Leon Garfield (Hodder & Stoughton). All offer short yet very

powerfully written descriptions that would usefully serve as models for young writers. Leon Garfield's images are created with sparse but striking language that will appeal to children. His use of repetition and simile in *Fair's Fair*, for example, could easily be transposed into children's writings through supported activities, and related to a range of other settings.

might want to suggest a range of possibilities. For example, the place could be dark and mysterious, bright and noisy, quiet and warm, cosy, compact, a wide-open space, airy, with a scent of the sea or snow or baking.

④ Now ask the children to write down the name of this place. It may already have its own name or they may choose to change it or they may need to invent one. The name may be a literal reflection of the place, for example 'White Castle Corner' or may offer a hint, such as 'Deadman's Lane'. With more experienced writers, this could develop into places that are misnamed or that deliberately deceive or give a false impression.

⑤ Invite the children to tell each other in pairs about their favourite place, using sufficient detail to create a strong visual image in their partner's mind and give a sense of their own enthusiasm about it. Remind them to use language to prompt their partner to imagine it as clearly as possible, helping them with what they can expect to see, hear, smell and so on. Try to give them some sense of how big or small things are and what they could reach and touch.

⑥ In shared writing, model how to create a strong image of a setting, using detailed and expressive vocabulary. Base this on your special space described at the beginning of the lesson, or a good example from the children. Brainstorm ideas, using headings of *What can I see? What can I hear? What can I smell? What do I feel?* to create the atmosphere. Using specific examples from the children, demonstrate how, with careful selection of language, brief descriptions can be built upon to create strong images, for example, changing *it is a big tree* to *it is a giant among trees*. Perhaps refer to Leon Garfield's use of repetition: *an old dead house, with an old dead door*. Draft

a paragraph to create an image of a scene that could be used to open a story. Refine some of the language used.

⑦ Give the children the opportunity to shape descriptive paragraphs of their own scene, using group members as critical friends.

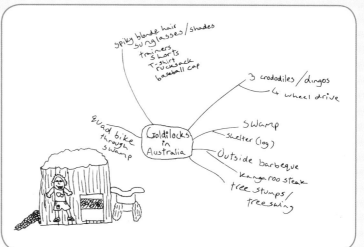

Moving on

● Provide the children with a range of pictures (these could be collected from travel brochures, magazine articles, fine art postcards) and ask them, in pairs, to select one to use as the setting for a story. Give the children time to compose two or three paragraphs describing the scene in the picture. Remind them that the written composition has to provide the reader with enough information to capture their imagination and enable them to picture the scene without the visual support. Other groups could then 'test' the description by reading or hearing it and working out which of the pictures is being described.

● This work on descriptive language could be further developed by a critical examination of a range of travel brochures. These could inspire the creation of a persuasive text, or simply to explore descriptions written to tempt readers and potential holidaymakers to visit certain destinations.

Change the setting

In this activity, the children are invited to retell a well-known story, placing it in a new setting. They will come to understand how the setting of a story influences other elements of the story, and they will enjoy reworking these to make their version of the story work. This kind of transformation is a process that writers all over the world have been doing for centuries. From Shakespeare to Tolstoy to the present day, stories have been remoulded, sometimes so the original story is barely recognisable. *King Lear*, for example, is said to be a Cinderella story!

What to do

❶ Agree with the children a story that they know very well and that they consider ripe for transformation. Read the story, or extracts from it that give details of the setting in place and time. Establish what these are with the children.

❷ Ask the children to brainstorm in pairs a few ideas for changing the setting for the story. They may choose to move it to a particular city in modern-day Britain or modern-day USA. They may choose an African village or Kingston, Jamaica; perhaps a French farm or Antarctic research station. They may wish the new time of the story to be in the future and even decide on a specific year – Red Riding Hood might now be set in 2012. You could write an example on the flipchart and discuss it with the children. How is this setting different? What implications does it have on the rest of

Literature links

A simple, but very clever example of this replacing is *Snow White in New York* by Fiona French. Many recent productions of Shakespeare plays on stage and screen have been updated to various eras of the 20th century, and Disney famously moved *Treasure Island* into space! Greek myths are great to transform to the modern world too. Try Geraldine McCaughrean's collection *The Orchard Book of Greek Myths*. Many old stories, such as traditional fairy tales, can be brought to the modern day in this way. 'The Old Woman in the Wood' on page 94 could be a good story to play around with. For example it might be turned into the 'Old Woman of the Housing Estate', a child sheltering in an abandoned flat, helped by another form of bird – a crow or a blackbird. It might be changed into a science fiction adventure set in space. Equally, new stories can be taken to historical periods in the past. What would *Bill's New Frock* by Anne Fine (Egmont) be like if the setting were changed to Tudor Britain? However the children decide to manipulate a story, they will need to know the original story well, and understand and be able to introduce the effects that changing the setting has on characters and events.

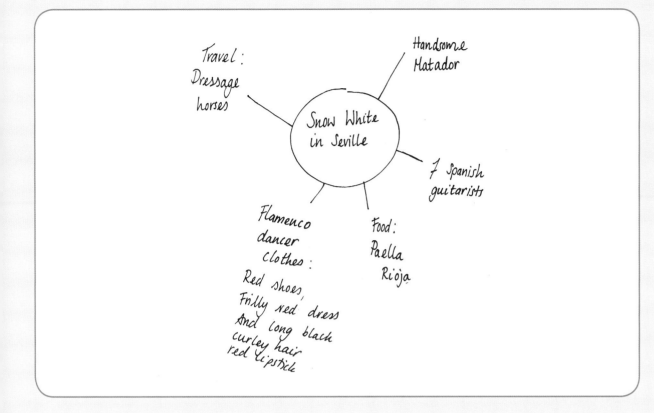

In the spider diagram:

- Travel: Dressage horses
- Handsome Matador
- Snow White in Seville
- 7 Spanish guitarists
- Food: Paella Rioja
- Flamenco dancer clothes: Red shoes, Frilly red dress And long black curley hair red lipstick

the story, including the characters? What clothes will the characters wear, for example? It may no longer be a Red Riding Hood, but some other form of head wear – an Islamic scarf, or an oxygen helmet, for example. How will they travel? What will they be eating? What kind of homes will they live in? A good way to collate these ideas is in the form of a simple spider diagram.

❸ Ask the children to continue to work in their pairs, doing this same process for their new setting. Suggest they use the same spider diagram form to note their ideas, as this can expand as they go along. Encourage them to share their thoughts, listening and working together to build on each other's ideas in a collaborative way. Tell them that when they are working in pairs like this they are said to be 'inter-thinking'.

❹ Before the children start to write the story in pairs, share some ideas to help those who are struggling a little. Guided writing would be a useful method of working on this activity. This enables

you to work with children with similar difficulties, or indeed to work with children who are very experienced writers who need to be extended in some way. For those who need greater support, the changes to the story may be quite simple, perhaps just concentrating on setting alone.

Moving on

● Invite the children to illustrate their new versions. Make a display of these or arrange a reading for other classes in the school.

● The children may like to research some of the detail of the new setting they are putting the story into. For example, if the setting looks back to a past time in this country, or to the present in another country, the inclusion of details gained from historical and geographical research would make their settings more complete, authentic, believable and interesting.

Preposition plays

This activity is a playful way to encourage children to make use of prepositions in composing pieces of writing that describe a setting for a story. It should be carried out in conjunction with work that has given children the opportunity to experience a range of literature with powerfully realised settings. It is important to emphasise that this does not mean providing short passages, isolated from their texts, but rather that children meet good setting descriptions within the context of reading whole texts. This activity deliberately exaggerates the use of prepositions in order to focus children's attention and understanding of their function.

Literature links

Reading fiction should always be about fun and rich enjoyment, so it is important that children should hear the whole story from which you are using extracts. One way of doing this is to draw on books that you have read recently as a class. Of course, short stories can also be used. Good writers will always use powerful settings to ignite the fire in their stories. Eoin Colfer's *Artemis Fowl* or Paul Jennings' *Unbelievable!* (both Puffin) are good at this in the fantasy genre, as well as Lesley Howarth's *Paulina* (Walker Books) – her setting here is rather creepy. An example of a longer classic text is Anna Sewell's *Black Beauty*, which has beautifully crafted descriptions of settings.

What to do

❶ If you feel children will initially have problems with this activity, choose a member of the class who could model the activity with you before you ask the children to try it in pairs. Decide upon a setting you would like to describe. It may be a setting typical of the particular genre you are currently studying. It could be a scary graveyard, it may be a massive football stadium or a wonderful enchanted garden or wood. Face your partner and make a statement that begins to describe the setting. Your partner must then continue the description you started. The only rule to follow is that each partner must begin his or her speech with a preposition. For example:

Partner 1 Beneath the yew trees that surrounded the graveyard, headstones jaggedly stuck through the earth like misshapen teeth.

Partner 2 Beside the graves lay the withered remains of yesterday's grief, the blooms of remembrance dead and scattered.

❷ Organise the children into pairs and ask them to discuss a setting they would like to describe. They should then face their partner and take turns to describe their setting, beginning with a preposition each time. This will be a challenge, but good fun, and should generate a range of descriptions.

© Derek Cooknell

③ Once the children have had a reasonable length of time to compose their description, encourage them to discuss the quality of what they have done. The children should ask each other whether they could see the place in their 'mind's eye'. When this happens, they can look at how this was made possible.

④ Invite one or two pairs to repeat their work for the rest of the class. This will give you the opportunity to praise descriptive and creative work and highlight aspects that are effective. It will also give you the chance to discuss the effect of the children's compositions upon the reader's visual construct of the setting. Encourage the children to give feedback too. Did they find it the activity difficult but fun? Did they find that thinking of a preposition first was a useful springboard for the rest of the sentence?

Moving on

● The partnerships could write up their oral work as part of a story that they then go on to write together. You might encourage them to attempt to mimic the style of a particular author in the genre they have been studying if this is appropriate to their choice of story setting.

● Including ICT will enhance writing that may come from this activity. Ask the children to illustrate their descriptions with pictures that are scanned in, perhaps created by the children themselves. They may wish to experiment with different sizes and types of fonts, even colours, that seem appropriate to their texts.

Video shorts

The purpose of this activity is to observe and identify the indicators of setting in the context of a film or television programme. A short section is selected for close examination, and the visual images, sounds, music and the interaction of the characters with the setting is examined. These video shorts can also be useful for comparing film and book versions of the same story and for exploring the similarities and differences in how settings are conveyed in these forms. This work can extend children's vocabulary for describing settings. It highlights the use of drawing on a reader's senses to evoke a powerful sense of the place and its interaction with the characters and events.

What to do

❶ Select a short passage (three to five minutes) from a video, which clearly depicts the setting and also shows how the setting influences the narrative action. For example, the scene in *Matilda* by Roald Dahl when Miss Honey and Matilda enter Miss Trunchbull's house to rescue the doll, they get locked in by the suspicious Miss Trunchbull who runs around the house with a baseball bat in search of them. The house itself feeds into the development of the plot, characters and general atmosphere.

❷ Discuss the story if it is not one you are currently reading and contextualise the chosen video extract for the class, by reading the passage prior to it or by recounting the events that have led up to this moment. If it is a book or film the children know, encourage them to work in pairs to remind one another of the story and its setting, for example, in *Matilda*, Miss Trunchbull's mansion, packed with mementoes of the past and reminders of her horrible nature.

❸ Watch the extract just once at first. Discuss the children's reactions to it – the atmosphere

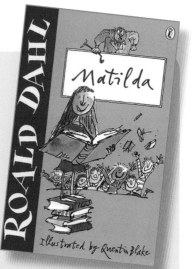

Literature links

A range of contemporary films can be used, ideally those that are well known by the children so they can appreciate the short clips in the context of the whole story. Suggestions might usefully include Disney's *The Lion King*, *Mulan*, *Peter Pan*, *The Little Mermaid* or *Aladdin*, which all have particularly colourful and evocative settings. In addition, you may wish to make links between children's literature (classic and otherwise) and available video material. Examples might include short sections from *The Lion, the Witch and the Wardrobe* by CS Lewis (Collins), *Black Beauty* by Anna Sewell (various publishers), *The Railway Children* by E Nesbit (various publishers), *Matilda* by Roald Dahl (Puffin) or one of JK Rowling's Harry Potter series in book (Bloomsbury) and film. Carefully selected scenes from these films can be used for direct comparison with passages in the written text.

Dark gloomy tomb.

crackled up cobwebs.

rugged walls.
stale damp disgusting smell.
creaking open of an old door.
footsteps echoing.
feeling scared from foot to head.
Wow! are they birds, butterflys, insects or magical fairys?
wizzing sounds like bees and humming birds.
Keys trying to slash me and slice me.
Wow! I'm scared, puzzled, I'm fascinated.

arrows making a machine gun noise.

shivery, cold, evil darkness.
old and danky.
smoky flames.
swords unsheathing like "shingggg!"

created, the feelings of the characters and the sense of place evoked.

❹ Watch the video short again, this time with the volume off. Explain to the children that after this you are going collect words to describe the setting.

❺ Ask the children to think of words and phrases that powerfully describe the setting, for example the *murderous* mansion in *Matilda* could be *an old house that shivered and quaked,* there could be *echoes* in the *emptiness* of the *cold rooms,* and an atmosphere of being imprisoned. List these ideas on the flipchart, recording them as 'premier, first or second division' phrases. This football metaphor is to help differentiate between more mundane and ordinary language and richer, more evocative imagery. Ask the children to help you categorise what is offered and encourage them to develop their ideas and improve their language to ensure they are placed in the premier league.

❻ Watch the video again, with the volume up, and focus on any of the senses that have not been fully used so far, for example, hearing, touch and taste. Again, list these in the divisions on the flipchart.

❼ In shared writing, create a paragraph that captures the setting in the video. Explain that you are working towards conveying a strong sense of the setting through the narrative action, *not* as a separate descriptive paragraph. Make use of at least four of the premier or first division ideas recorded, and model ways to integrate the setting into the action. Notice how the sense of place can be contextualised and brought to life through the action, for example, in *Matilda*, in the tense chase around the house:

As the glass chandelier swung precariously above her, Matilda's heart raced in her thin chest. 'Miss Honey?' she whispered frantically. The old house shivered and quaked; it too was afraid. Matilda's words echoed ominously around the room. Her eyes fell upon a set of baseball bats displayed on the far wall, the lock was undone... one was missing. As she slipped silently into the hall Matilda noticed with alarm that the curtains were flapping even though the windows were shut tight. She was imprisoned in a living nightmare. Where was Miss Trunchbull?

❽ Challenge the children to write their own paragraph, making use of at least three different premier league phrases.

Moving on

● If you have chosen a dramatisation of a book, read out the written version of the episode and examine the language chosen to convey the sense of the place and the atmosphere as well as its interaction with the participants.

● Make a wall display with premier league and first division phrases, adding to this over time and reminding the children that the setting can also be depicted through action and is not always offered as a solitary descriptive passage.

Guess the setting

This activity supports children in identifying characters and settings and matching the two. This will help them as they lean on conventions and apply appropriate language and linguistic devices when they create settings to match characters. It will also encourage the development of skills necessary to subvert these conventions as they become more confident writers and seek to juxtapose settings and characters in unconventional ways. The activity will also develop their ability to describe stories critically.

What to do

❶ Organise the children to work in pairs. Ask one child from each pair to choose one book from the collection that contains an illustration of a key character in the story.

❷ Without showing the other child the picture or the book (sitting back to back might be best for this) the child with the

Literature links

Because an image as well as a strong main character is needed for this activity, stories that best support it will generally be in picture fiction, such as John Steptoe's *Mufaro's Beautiful Daughters* (Puffin). Illustrated traditional tales will also be useful, for example *The Boy and the Cloth of Dreams* by Jenny Koralek (Walker Books), or those in Stories to Tell in this book.

book should describe the character in detail, for example *I'm looking at a girl who is wearing...*

❸ From this description, the partner should try to guess where and when the story is set. The child with the book can give more clues from the character's appearance, bearing and behaviour.

❹ Ask the children then to swap roles, with the other child choosing a picture from a different story, and repeat the activity.

❺ Having created a rough oral description of the two settings, ask the pairs to choose one to develop into a short written paragraph. Encourage the children to collaborate on writing, reading through and editing.

Moving on

● Some of the children could read their descriptive paragraphs to the class and the rest of the children could guess where the story is set and attempt to match it to the book in the collection.

● The children could incorporate their descriptive paragraph into the beginnings of a new story. They could continue this in pairs, or work individually, which would then make for an interesting comparison of the different stories created with the same setting and main character.

Chapter Four

Theme and Language

In examining and exploring the themes and language of stories, teachers can make use of the range of open-ended activities suggested here. The premise behind these activities is the recognition that there are many possible responses to any form of fiction. The children are encouraged to form personal engagements with stories and to develop the expression and support of their views with reference to the details of the stories being examined.

Theme

Children of this age group will be developing their ability both to discuss themes, and to compose texts of their own that have a particular chosen theme. Analysis of theme can becomes more in-depth and children can begin to introduce 'hidden' meanings, world views and underlying messages into their own story writing. Theme is perhaps the most personal literary element of a story, as it asks readers to consider what the story means to them on several levels, and prompts them to relate the narrative and its issues to their own lives.

Many contemporary stories and poems raise issues, that deal challengingly with a particular social theme such as bullying. A theme like this is often highly visible and easily defined, for example *The Angel of Nitshill Road* by Anne Fine (Egmont), *The Bully* by Jan Needle (Puffin), *Bully* by David Hughes (Walker Books) and the poem 'The Bully' by Berlie Doherty in her anthology *Walking on Air* (Lions).

Such themes can be explored sensitively but effectively in a number of ways: through drama and discussion, through short stories that focus on the issue in a different but complementary manner. Problem–resolution tales that have one central dilemma provide a useful structure for children to emulate when they are attempting to write a story with a clear theme. In addition, it is worth comparing several authors' treatment of a similar theme.

Short stories, and in particular picture books that encourage close observation and reading beyond the literal, are helpful for exploring themes, particularly tales written and/or illustrated by Anthony Browne, Michael Foreman and Colin Thompson as these authors often highlight their themes clearly. For example, in *Changes* by Anthony Browne (Walker Books) there is a new baby in the family; in *The Paperbag Prince* by Colin Thompson (Red Fox), the focus is clearly on the environment; in Thompson's *Falling Angels* (Red Fox), it is on dreams and belief.

Identifying themes in traditional tales can also be worthwhile, as such tales deal, sometimes in quite 'black and white' ways, with archetypal issues about the human condition. These can provide useful models, particularly for children who may struggle to

keep consistency and a sense of progress in writing stories with more complex themes. Traditional stories often incorporate contrasts and include, for example:

- a journey from poverty to wealth (whether materially or spiritually)
- wisdom and foolishness
- the young and the old
- tests of an individual's strength or humanity
- weakness and strength
- the beautiful and the ugly
- a journey as a symbol of self-discovery.

These universal themes are not carried through the plot alone, but are invested in the characters – their development, the predicaments they face and often in their journeys through life. The metaphorical nature of the language in such stories also carries the theme, creating clearly contrasting characters whose motivation, behaviour, speech and feelings often highlight the theme and enable children to make connections to their lives.

Language

The language of stories, whether expressed in the first or third person, creates the tune on the page and the voice and verve of the telling. The choice of language and style of writing is important, and children need to hear, read, study and experience a wide range of such voices. Focusing on prolific authors such as David Almond, Philippa Pearce, Jan Mark, Sharon Creech, Michael Morpurgo, Berlie Doherty or Gillian Cross enables the children to examine and define an author's style. Books for guided reading as well as independent reading and shared work can be drawn from these authors' works. Good examples of vivid use of language in novels include:

- *Skellig* and *Kit's Wilderness* – David Almond (Hodder)
- *Out of the Ashes* (Macmillan) and *Kensuke's Kingdom* (Egmont) – Michael Morpurgo
- *The Dark Behind the Curtain* – Gillian Cross (OUP)
- *Wolf* – Gillian Cross (Puffin)
- *Journey to the River Sea* – Eva Ibbotson (Macmillan)
- The *Edge Chronicles* series by Paul Stewart (Corgi).

Traditional tales, in their various incarnations, are again a valuable resource for studying story language. A selection is offered in Stories to Tell in this book. These stories often have distinctive plot patterns marked by repetitive and memorable language, rich with metaphor and imagery, and often humour. Traditional openings and endings as well as rhythmic refrains and repeated phrases are also common in this genre. Such tales were originally moulded for the ear and many still retain considerable rhythm, resonance and repetition. The direct and lively language of some oral stories is echoed in written versions, while others have a more poetic and evocative style.

The opportunity to compare and contrast language and styles in old and modern versions of traditional tales is available with the wealth of retellings and parodies on the market. Powerful picture book retellings in which the language sings, the literary style is marked and the illustrations add to the text

© Photodisc, Inc.

are also well worth exploring with children of this age, who are not always encouraged to explore picture stories any more. Particularly strong writers in this genre are Kevin Crossley-Holland, Geraldine McCaughrean and Jane Yolen and works illustrated by Chris Riddell. Good examples for study include:

- *Beauty and the Beast* – Geraldine McCaughrean (Picture Corgi)
- *Nobody Rides the Unicorn* – Adrian Mitchell (Picture Corgi)
- *Rapunzel* – Paul O Zelinsky (Puffin)
- *Thief in the Village* – James Berry (Puffin)
- *Enchantment* – Kevin Crossley-Holland (Orion)
- *The Merrymaid of Zennor* – Charles Causley (Orchard)
- *The Birdman* – Melvin Burgess (Andersen Press).

Reading journals

> My favourite book.
>
> My favourite book is Goodnight Mister Tom. I like this book because it connects with me. It shows me what life is like in a safe warm home compared to a house which is warstruck. After reading it though you start to feel extremely sorry for will and you will wonder how he feels and how he managed to survive in his Mums house. I've really thought that this book took me inside it and showed me what life was like during world war two. One of the best bits is when he's locked in the cupboard because the vivid description really involves you in wills feelings and thoughts.

On a regular basis, let the children briefly write an entry in their reading journals, formulating a response to current reading. Creating intertextual links will support the sense of analysis and will draw attention to theme and language. Through this activity, children will develop personal responses and articulate them in discussion. It will help them to write summaries, commentaries and reviews. As they become more experienced in scrutinising texts, they will become more discriminating about those they choose to read, re-read and recommend.

Literature links

It would be helpful in the initial stages to draw attention to where themes or genres of texts are similar, but it is important that children have ownership of this practice and can make independent choices.

What to do

❶ The success of this activity depends on ample time for reading, reflection and writing about a story that the children enjoyed or found meaningful. They also need regular opportunities to talk about the books. The reading journals will offer an agenda for this.

❷ Model a structure for the children. You could identify a character, a setting or an event that resonates and explain why this is the case. For example, *the description of the rocky coast in* Daughter of the Sea *reminds me of holidays in Cornwall...* Using response partners can be a useful rehearsal before writing journal entries and sharing them later.

❸ Although it may be important for the journal to have an audience, which may be you or a friend, it is not appropriate to assess the entries, but rather to respond to them in a personal way. For example, you might reply to the above example by agreeing and offering a further connection, perhaps to a television programme that offers a similar visual image, or relate it to another text that the class have shared. Other comments may reflect particular aspects of the response – *I felt frightened at that part too!*

❹ The most straightforward way to structure the journal initially would be by making chronological entries, but as the children become more experienced they may decide to construct subsequent journals in genre sections, or to colour code them.

Moving on

● Offering critical responses in a debate forum would support the children in developing this ability to articulate their appreciation and support their judgements.

Form exchange

One Wicked Witch!

Now this is a story all about how
one witch got turned r-r-right upside down,
She roast her b-butt on a roaring flame,
now thats what I call one wicked d-dame!

YO!

Gingerbread, sugarplums, candy too,
Hansel and Grettal in a forest of yew,
that chicken bone tricked the red-eyed crone,
She fell for that trick,
Yo Hansel, you s-s-s-slick!

In this activity, children use the differences between two forms of text to explore meaning and language. They experiment with prose and poetry in which the form has been changed from what would normally be expected. In doing so, they will discover how the choosing of a genre and form as a vehicle for the meaning can be an important aspect of the writing process.

What to do

❶ Make sure the children have discussed stylistic and linguistic devices used in raps and performed some of their own.

Literature links

Many forms of writing can be converted into others. Traditional ballads can be converted to raps, poems into plain chant or prose. Why not convert a fairy story into a rap? The children will appreciate having a wide selection of new and familiar tales to choose from and will have fun with putting an old story into a modern form. For useful example texts and inspiration, try Shel Silverstein's *Falling Up* (Collins), or Michael Rosen's collection *The Kingfisher Book of Children's Poetry*. Many of these texts can be changed into prose form and still have significant impact on readers. 'The Jester and the King' (page 82) would also suit a conversion. Tony Mitton's 'Little Red Riding Hood' rap from his book *Big Bad Raps* (Orchard) is a good example of changing forms.

❷ Read a traditional version of your chosen story, for example 'Little Red Riding Hood', then read or listen to a modern verse or rap version, such as that by Tony Mitton.

❸ Enjoy the differences in language, rhythm and style. Notice if the essence of the characters and plot remain the same.

❹ In shared writing, recap the plot of the story. Then, as you go back to focus on each significant event or description, begin to convert the story into rap. 'Little Red Riding Hood', for example might start:

There was a girl called Little Red Hood
Didn't walk the path she knew she should.

❺ Ask the children to work in pairs to compose a rap from their own choice of fairy story. Give them space and time to rap it out loud, during and after writing.

Moving on

● The children will enjoy performing the raps to each other and other children in the school. You could add instruments to make the performances really lively. Draw up a 'set list' to perform and schedule a tour around the school.

● For a 'converse' activity, read the children a narrative poem and ask them to make it into prose. Try 'The Highwayman' by Alfred Noyes.

Page **67**

Cartoon names

The purpose of this activity is to examine the names of characters in comics and cartoons to identify ways in which names and titles can be used to indicate the content and themes of a story. This will support the children as they begin to use such authorial devices from their own stories and select models from traditional children's literature and popular cultural texts, such as comics/cartoon strips. Children are asked to work through the whole writing process, from planning through to presentation, so the activity will take more than one session to complete. The children will enjoy this activity and you should find that their engagement with texts from their leisure-time activities inspires great creativity.

Literature links

Compile a collection of suitable story comics and cartoons. *The Beano* would be useful because it is not age specific nor is it gender focused and is sufficiently funny to engage the children. *The Dandy* is another 'oldie but goldie', but look for computer game, television-based or film tie-in comics too, like *Sonic the Comic*, *Nickelodeon*, *Looney Tunes* and *Wickid*, and adventures of Spider Man and the X-Men. You could also look at longer cartoon stories, such as those by Marcia Williams', or look at books on Asterix, Tintin and Calvin and Hobbes. At this level, the children will feel at ease in taking risks and engaging playfully with this activity. Before you start, you could ask for a comic/ magazine 'amnesty', creating an opportunity for children to bring comics in from home. Children will often have a huge pile of discarded comics tucked away under the bed or stuffed in drawers. Take advantage of this! Another way to maintain a steady supply of such material is to ask the literacy co-ordinator to set up a subscription to some popular suitable titles.

What to do

❶ Provide boxes of comics from which the children, in pairs, can select one or two. Ask the children then to select particular cartoons or comic strips from these and identify the ways in which the name of the strip (usually also the name of the main character) reflects the content or general tone of the story (for example 'Beryl the Peril' or 'Dennis the Menace').

❷ Take one example from the comics box yourself to question ways in which the story content marries with the name of the key character. For example, ask *How is Dennis a menace in his stories? What does he do that causes him to get his name? How does his name indicate what sort of thing might go on in the story?* By asking these kind of questions you raise the possibility of discussing the theme of morality, for example, and if those perpetrating 'foul deeds' in the story receive their comeuppance. Ask the children to list three ways that their chosen character's name influences the theme, language, plot and tone (humorous, for instance) of the story.

③ Continuing in pairs, ask the children to use these models to brainstorm possible names for their own cartoon characters. Tell them to choose two or three from their brainstorm initially and identify how they could make these character names impact on the story content. From this second stage, fuller ideas for a story should be working away in the children's thoughts and they should be able to whittle their choice of character down to the one that seems to have the most promise in terms of character and story development and expression of theme.

④ The story can be written from this, following cartoon style frames initially, if appropriate. Provide the children with a blank cartoon-strip 'template' and let the children fill the frames, storyboard style, with the ideas they have devised so far for their story.

⑤ Once the children have made their, predominantly visual, cartoon strip, they could discuss possible dialogue and descriptions suitable for each frame before getting down to writing in a more

traditional style. This oral rehearsal is a useful way for children to experiment with the vocabulary they can use.

Moving on

● This activity could be adapted by inviting the children to look at character names and story titles in books rather than comics and cartoons, for example *James and the Giant Peach, The BFG* (both Puffin) or many other Roald Dahl texts. They could then invent character names for their own stories and make a character sketch in which they indicate how the characteristics link with the theme they are presenting in the story.

● The children could use this device in a different way by creating a character sketch and inviting other children to suggest a name for the character. Once a name has been agreed, the group could then decide what kind of story the character would be in and the kind of themes running through it.

Thinking about themes

The purpose of this activity is to help children build up a repertoire of themes to use in their stories and develop their personal responses to stories they hear and read. The children will draw parallels between stories, make intertextual references and notice authorial devices that they can employ as writers. To introduce children to this work, encourage them to identify themes in a popular, published novel before they begin to construct their own. After reading, a visual stimulus in the form of 'theme wheels' will give the children a starting point and encourage them to focus on this story element.

Literature links

This activity suits stories that contain layers of meaning so that the children can make thematic connections at their own level and based on their own experience. Initially, it works best if the children know the story to some degree. These books all offer rich opportunities to study theme at this level:

- *Farm Boy* (HarperCollins) and *The Wreck of the Zanzibar* (Egmont) – Michael Morpurgo
- *Daughter of the Sea* (Puffin) and *White Peak Farm* (Mammoth) – Berlie Doherty
- *Skellig, Kit's Wilderness* and *Heaven Eyes* (all Hodder) – David Almond.

What to do

❶ Recap a known story or read out a short story, and ask for the children's responses to it. Combine some of the more basic questions with those that require a deeper response from the children. Ask, for example:

- Where is the story set? Do you know a place like this?
- What is the story about? (Develop this to be more than just plot – *What point of view is the author putting across? What is the meaning at the heart of the story?*)
- Are the characters believable? Which is the most likeable? Why? Do they remind you of anyone you know? In what ways?
- Did you enjoy the story? What in particular? How did it make you feel?
- How would you describe the story? (For example, exciting, tense, scary, strange, haunting, tender, heart-warming.)
- Does it remind you of any other stories?

❷ Give the children time to discuss this further in pairs, then collect views on the flipchart. As the pairs are sharing their thoughts, ask them to provide examples from the text to support their ideas.

❸ Talk about the wide range of responses given and discuss why our personal experiences, preferences, interests and points of view will help us as readers to determine what the story means to us as individuals. As an example to help make this point, briefly create a disparate set of characters for a book group and help the children to see how each of those members will respond differently to the themes of one text.

❹ Using your notes on the flipchart, ask the children to identify the range of themes that have been noted in your chosen story. In *Skellig*, for example, these could be family, religion, life and death, fear of death, love, growing up, magic, beliefs.

❺ Using the same text, work as a class to put the themes in a hierarchical order, from the most powerful to more minor aspects. It would be useful at this stage to explore with the class how some of these themes work together and how they are developed through the text.

❻ Using three large concentric circles, made from card and fixed in the middle with a split pin and arrow, write some of the themes the children have chosen around the edges of the two largest circles. Around the small circle write suggestions for characters, for example: a mother, a father, a child, a mysterious character, a baby and so on. If at this stage you wish to expand the children's experience towards the creation of new stories or extensions, then other characters could be introduced, for example a witch, two boys, a grandmother and so on.

❼ Ask each pair of children to spin the wheels and, where the circles line up at the arrowhead, think of how the character might be involved with those themes, providing suggestions for the beginning of a story.

Love

Life and death

Magic

Growing up

Baby

Child

Mother

Family

Father

Religion

Beliefs

Fear of death

❽ Ask the pairs to note down the ideas from their discussion so that some examples can be shared. Explore how, for example, similar themes have been introduced through different characters.

Moving on

● Using a single visual image (unrelated to any text; perhaps an art poster or a photograph from a travel brochure), ask the children in small groups to brainstorm ideas for themes that emerge from it. Share these and discuss how several themes and story ideas can be drawn from one source.

● Invite children to develop their stories by 'borrowing' a theme from another group and adding it to their own so that their stories become double layered. For example, one group may have talked about 'generations' as a theme, then borrow 'life and death' from another group. It should prove a worthwhile challenge to continue their story with this additional theme in mind.

Film themes

This activity encourages children to study recurring themes in certain genres of stories, using films as the texts to analyse. It is a quick activity that can be carried out within a unit of work. It encourages collaborative work and allows children to create graphic representations of key themes. What will provide extra interest and stimulation will be the use of popular film texts instead of books. Most modern films made for children can be categorised into story types just as books can. In film, just as in books, themes such as the struggle between good and evil, friendship, romantic love, the powerful defeated by the weak, innocence, and corruption, can be identified with particular text types. This activity invites children to hunt for these themes and pull them out for scrutiny, including some that are questionable in terms of, for example, sexism or racism. For older children the identification of stereotypes and simplistic points of view can be a valuable exercise.

What to do

❶ Model the activity, using clips from a well-known film. Refreshingly, the screen here replaces the book and gives a new perspective to 'shared reading'. Introduce the film and encourage the children to discuss it – the characters, plot, setting and themes. This will whet the children's appetite for the activity and you will notice the sudden engagement with the Literacy Hour!

❷ Explain that you are going to record themes on the flipchart in the form of a spider diagram. Write the name of the film in the centre of the flipchart and begin to list around it the themes that the children have identified. You may want to suggest to the children that they note these down as they notice them while they are watching the film. *Jungle Book* has friendship, kindness to others and belonging as main themes that run through the film. The battle between good and evil is also a theme of this film.

Literature links

Films can be a very immediate and involving way of identifying and analysing the themes of stories. Try to collect a stock of videos or DVDs of films the children are likely to have seen. Disney's *The Jungle Book* is a film that encourages viewers to challenge the themes presented. A main theme is friendship and familial care. Another recurring theme is belonging somewhere, both having a sense of this yourself and where others think that you should belong. There is a place for the animals in the jungle and a place for Mowgli, in the 'man village'. The final scene shows a young girl singing a happy song about her place being married to a man who hunts in the jungle while she cooks the food in the kitchen. Disney retellings of fairy tales have all the thematic material of the written texts on which they are based, for example *Snow White and the Seven Dwarfs* and *Cinderella*. DreamWorks' *Shrek*, and in some ways, Universal Pictures' *The Grinch*, parody many of the themes found in traditional fairy stories and children of this age should be able to appreciate the 'in' jokes and layers of humour. *Shrek* is a great film to use at the end of a unit of work on traditional tales, as it both celebrates and mocks the tales we all know so well.

Alternatively, once the themes have been suggested, you could then make that the centre of your flipchart diagram and record where this theme comes out.

❸ Ask the children in pairs or threes to choose a film they know well. In the same way, ask them to recall and discuss the plot, characters, setting and work to make their spider diagram of the themes that can be found in the film.

❹ At the end of the session ask the children to attach their posters to the wall with Blu-Tack. Allow the other children to browse what their peers have done. This will make a change from the normal plenary of show and tell.

❺ When the children are settled again, pull out particular observations that reinforce the learning about theme and meaning. Offer comments on some of the films and the themes you found interesting, then invite the children to do the same. The children can comment on each other's

work, drawing on their knowledge of the film that their friends have chosen. They can debate whether or not they agree and a forum is opened up that allows polite debate and the sharing of ideas.

Moving on

● Ask the children to use their spider diagrams to write a story with similar themes. Settings, characters and plot can be changed, but the themes need to be preserved. As you have been using film for this activity, you may wish to ask children to think up the setting, characters and plot of a new film that will explore similar themes. This will make a change from the formal writing of a story, but will teach the same objectives. The children could then storyboard the opening sequence of the film. A storyboard for a film shows the key shots from a particular scene rather like a comic strip.

Yes, no, why

This activity develops views about the language of stories and enables children to assert their perspective, justifying with reference to the purpose and nature of the text. It is a valuable activity in shared or guided reading, and can also contribute to children's awareness of the options and choices available to and taken by authors. Over time, and in the context of other language work, the learning from this activity will enrich their writing.

What to do

❶ If possible, copy out your chosen passage into the middle of A3 sheets to allow room for the children's annotations in the margins. Try to choose a passage that is particularly evocative of a character or setting, but avoid merely descriptive passages; if some element of narrative is involved, this will support the discussion.

❷ Frame the activity by re-reading passages and discussing the story so far. For

example, in chapter 9 of *The Seeing Stone*, Kevin Crossley-Holland reflects upon the hill and the sinister black mountains in the distance. The young Arthur knows instinctively that one day he will travel west to the mountains, and this passage acts as a premonition of things to come.

❸ Read the first sentence of the chosen passage and ask the children for their immediate reactions. Do they like it? Dislike it? Does it remind them of anywhere/anyone/anything? What hints about the rest of the text are offered? The particular questions you ask which the children could consider briefly in pairs, will depend upon the extract. What is important is that you give space for connections to be made with the rest of the story and with other texts, and that thoughts can be prompted through informal conversation with peers. Although the focus is on language, don't direct children to particular metaphors or details, but let them follow *their* interests and observations, then consider together

Literature links

The children should examine extracts from quality literature, but these must be contextualised. For example, your extract choices may include a passage from the current class novel or from a short story or picture book that is going to be read in full by the children. The extract needs to be potentially rich in relation to discussion of the language, but sufficiently far into the narrative to ensure the children are hooked by the storyline and the characters' predicament. Its length will depend upon the book concerned – more is not necessarily better. Good examples

because of their rich, demanding language with use of figurative and metaphorical techniques include:

● *Counting Stars* – David Almond (Hodder)
● *The Rope and Other Stories* – Philippa Pearce (Puffin)
● *Falling Angels* – Colin Thompson (Red Fox)
● *Journey to the River Sea* – Eva Ibbotson (Macmillan)
● Kevin Crossley-Holland's Arthur trilogy (Orion), or his picture books for older juniors, such as *Sea Tongue* (BBC).

how the imagery or sense of tension or wonder is achieved.

④ Repeat the exercise with the second or third sentences, once again sharing their views, focusing on choices and, for example, on the evocative combinations of images created.

⑤ Read the rest of the text, then hand out copies and ask the children to read the whole passage for themselves. Ask them to identify sentences or phrases that they like. Invite them to record their views around the edge of the sheet, underlining the lines they like in a particular colour. Ask them to give reasons for their opinions as part of their annotations, so both the response and the appreciation of the chosen effect are recorded.

⑥ Share some examples of these. Gently probe further why the children have chosen these passages. What was it about the language, the images, their personal connections to it that prompted them to select this and warm to it?

⑦ Now focus on passages, lines or words, that, for whatever reason, they do not like or are puzzled about. Invite them to

This reminds me of the dungeons at Dover Castle

really descriptive

I like the moonlight

Something scary is about to happen

that is how I would feel

this is really spooky

underline these in different colours and note and discuss their views with their partners. Can they suggest richer alternatives? Some children might comment that repeating *violet hills* three times, for example, is unnecessary. Why might Kevin Crossley-Holland have done this? What else could he have written?

⑧ Again, share examples and encourage the children to talk about their reasons. Explain that all readers are entitled to their own perspective and all views are valid, and that some readers will, for a variety of reasons, find certain words and phrases less appealing, strange, or simply confusing. This discussion is likely to revolve initially around language that is difficult for some to understand – make sure you invite others to comment. Focus your discussion on the nature of the text, its purpose and likely audience, possible reasons for the author's choices, issues of clarity and inference and deduction.

Moving on

● You could encourage the children to develop the habit of identifying aspects of paragraphs, chapters and whole books that they don't feel are as powerful as others. Children find this hard and need to be encouraged to critically evaluate professional writers' work, justifying their views and articulating their perspective. This enables them over time to become more discerning readers who read, respond and reflect upon writers' language choices, considering their value, impact and effect more critically.

● You might want to try the same activity, moving paragraph by paragraph through the passage, so that everyone is focusing on the same piece of language. This is simpler and more focused, but does not achieve the same diversity as self-selection.

Life connections

Teachers of literacy will find that one of their main goals must be to help children build bridges between the themes and events in books and those in their own lives. As readers and writers, children need to access prior knowledge that will enable them to make meaning from the elements of stories. This activity encourages children to activate their own connections with stories, a process that will give them a reading strategy for life. In addition, by generating the understanding of the need for readers to connect with the elements of stories, this activity helps to give potential story writers the knowledge to be aware of their readership and to include the kind of elements that their readers will be able to understand.

What to do

❶ Read a story that you enjoy and that explores particular themes the children can relate to, for example a story from Dick King-Smith's *Friends and Brothers*. Stop after every page, or other convenient 'break', and say how you are connecting with the story on a personal level. It might refer to an argument you had with a sibling or the relationship with your parents; it may be a game that you would play or something you would do after you had your tea as a child. Articulate this kind of connection by saying, for example, *This reminds me of... or I remember when..., This event in the story makes me think of..., It makes me feel that..., Something like that happened to*

Literature links

Stories with themes connected to family life will encourage the children to relate directly with them. These texts will highlight the point that is being made in this activity about books needing to enable their readership to connect with their themes. Dick King-Smith's *Friends and Brothers* (Mammoth) is a collection of stories about two brothers and their life together. Ann Cameron's *The Julian Stories* (Yearling) explores the same themes, also using two brothers in their domestic setting. Shaun Tan's picture books *The Lost Thing* and *The Red Tree* (Lothian Publishing) explore themes of alienation in the modern world. School stories also share common themes: Judy Blume's *Blubber* (Pan), Robert Cormier's *The Chocolate*

War (Puffin) and Anne Fine's *The Angel of Nitshill Road* (Egmont) raise issues of bullying and school life in different ways. Also have available favourite books from the children's reading earlier in their lives, for example picture books like *Owl Babies* by Martin Waddell and *We're Going on a Bear Hunt* by Michael Rosen (both Walker Books).

me once. Encourage the children to relate the story to their own lives too, so a discussion is set up.

❷ Show the children a variety of different books written for different age groups of children, such as *Owl Babies* by Martin Waddell. The children will remember these books with fondness from their early years. Then hold up books from the children's current reading, such as books by Shaun Tan and Ann Cameron's books about Julian and Huey.

❸ Ask the children to categorise the books roughly by age level, then ask them to pick out similar themes and elements that the books have, looking for connections within the age groups. These may be stories about siblings, anxieties, joy, good and bad, and so on. List these on the flipchart, and help the children to see how the common themes are suitable for children of the particular age.

❹ Tell the children that they will be working in pairs to write stories for different age ranges within the school. Their stories will explore the appropriate themes they have identified and have elements that children of that age will relate to. Ask the pairs to discuss and decide on an age group to write for and what themes they want to include. (Alternatively, allocate the age ranges to the pairs if you want a fairly even spread.)

❺ Remind the children of work you may have done so far on building a story around a theme or incorporating a theme into a developing story. You will need to allow the children enough time to hold discussions in pairs, perhaps including a creative brainstorm, and to work their way through the writing process of planning, drafting, editing for meaning and effect, proof-reading and presentation.

© Derek Cooknell

❻ Arrange for the children to read their work to the target audience. The stories can then be included in the class collections.

Moving on

● Give children access to ICT to bring in clip art and a range of fonts to help create texts suitable for the age group they have chosen. Alternatively, they could illustrate their stories with their own drawings or paintings.

● Children could test out their stories in draft form to their target audience around the school and elicit opinions about their work so far. To develop this, they could encourage the children they are working with to share similar incidents and events that have happened in their lives. Allow the children follow-up writing time in which they can edit these ideas and comments into their stories.

Telling down

The purpose of this activity is twofold: firstly to focus on enriching the language of a story through a detailed retelling of one part of it, and also to provide an opportunity for the children to evaluate their own and each other's work in terms of composition and effect. In 'telling down' into the depths of a story, children will be working to convey feelings, reflections and mood in the description of characters, place (the setting or various settings) and the various incidents and events and dialogue. In evaluating good examples of stories the children will be involved in commenting critically on the language, style, adaptation and evocation of the chosen moment. This activity helps children as readers and future writers to get down into a story, fully using their imaginations to see the themes and meanings behind the characters and the narrative as presented. The children look at details 'missing' from the story in order to infer what might be happening or what the motives are behind certain events, dialogue and behaviour. This will help them to appreciate as writers that there is interaction between writer and reader and that details do not always need to be given, allowing the reader to bring their own ideas, experiences and inferences to the text, thus generating greater involvement and enjoyment.

What to do

❶ Use a simple percussion instrument or other framing device to mark the opening of the storytelling and to lend a bit of drama to the reading then read or tell your chosen story to the children.

❷ Afterwards, give the children a few moments to reflect on the story and, silently to themselves, choose a favourite part. This part may be an unnerving or highly exciting section, a moment of tension, a particularly intriguing description of a place. Then ask the children to tell a partner which part they chose and discuss why.

❸ Now ask the children to imagine that as a class they are going to break up the story into parts. Invite each child to think of and record a subtitle for his or her chosen

Literature links

Oral and traditional stories, myths, legends, folk and fairy tales are the most suitable for telling down, for example 'The Weaving of a Dream (page 84) and 'How the Sun Came into the World' (page 90). Lyrical versions of traditional takes such as the beautifully illustrated *Beauty and the Beast* by Geraldine McCaughrean (Picture Corgi), and *Sophie and the Sea Wolf* by Helen Cresswell (Hodder) are suitable to give as examples of this type of language use. This activity will work best with a more simple story that you are able to retell in one session, rather than just read.

© Derek Cooknell

favourite part. As an example, you could make your own choice of favourite section from the story, giving your reasons, and give it a suitable subtitle. Remind the children that a subtitle should be an attractive phrase that gives, in a succinct way, a summary or at least some indication of what its text is about. Examine these subtitles and favourite sections as a class, commenting on the variety of moments identified and discussing any patterns noticeable in the type of moment chosen or in the way the subtitles are composed.

❹ Remind the children of your choice of extract and explain that now you are going to 'tell it down'. Essentially, this means that you will be retelling just this section of the story in such a way that you expand upon it, offering more details of the setting, the characters' perspectives, the themes and so on to reveal underlying images. For example, in 'The Weaving of a Dream', the youngest son Leje travels over Flame Mountain but little detail is given

about this. In telling down this section you could describe the burning bushes, the billowing smoke and the hot volcanic lava trickling down the paths. Leje's heart was no doubt beating fast, his throat dry and his lips cracked. Did he falter, turn back briefly and then renew his resolve to rescue his mother's brocade? What images and thoughts came into his head, what precious memories returned to support him as he rode through the flames and felt the heat sear into his flesh? Did the stone horse resist? Did the saddle slip? What words unspoken were on the tip of his tongue? Enjoy spinning the yarn and describing the images you can see in your mind's eye.

❺ Ask the children to engage in orally 'telling down' into the hidden depths of their chosen section of the story, giving their subheadings as the title of their retelling of this mini-story. This oral storytelling works best in pairs, the partners having selected different moments in the tale.

6 Invite the children to comment upon each other's stories. Which images or ideas surprised their partner or were particularly evocative? Were there certain phrases that conjured up strong visual pictures? Can these be recalled and repeated? Did their partner build up suspense in actions as well as words? Which were the most amusing or frightening sections of the telling down? This oral feedback will support the children in the development of the second telling down exercise.

7 Organise the children to find new partners and in this 'storybuzz' time, ask them to take another chance to tell down into the story, then listen to their new partner's telling down. Encourage the children to incorporate their first partners' suggestions into this 'edited' retelling.

8 Now ask the children to write up their chosen section as one lengthy paragraph. Remind them to include their subtitle. These should then be exchanged with another partner, whose role it is to make written comments upon the composition, effects, language, themes and other elements as appropriate to the particular section of the story.

9 Share some of the paragraphs and the evaluative comments made. Working still further in this 'micro' way, perhaps ask for suggestions how the particular phrase, or word could be improved.

Moving on

● You might want the children to compare their in-depth retelling with the few sparse words given in the source material or your retelling of it. This could produce a fruitful discussion about quantity and quality, the differences between oral and written versions of the same tale and the influence of such detail upon the story. To develop this, encourage the children to find versions of traditional tales that contain good examples of detailed descriptive and evocative passages and literal and figurative language, and compare them with more 'simplistic', straightforward versions. What is the effect? How does each style fit the particular author's intentions (for example in generating humour, being subversive, applying a very modern feel or maintaining a serious, historical, traditional tone)?

● Combine various 'telling downs' from the children to recreate the story, inviting the children to fill any gaps. This lengthier version could then be compared with the original written version and the strengths and weaknesses, effects and potential purpose of both identified.

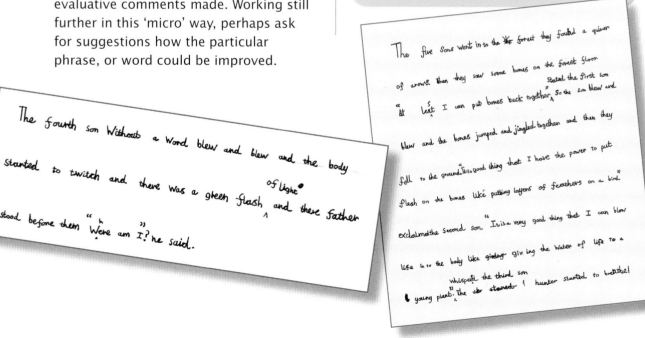

Stories to Tell

The Jester and the King

A Polish story

It had been for many years that Matenko had been the court jester for the King and Queen of Poland. His job was to entertain the tables of the court with jokes, funny stories, juggling, somersaults and general merry making. But Matenko was no longer a young man. His jokes were old, his stories ancient and his increasing rheumatism was reducing his ability to turn somersaults. The King and Queen looked at each other with despair when their friends and family didn't want to sit and listen to old Matenko anymore.

The situation was doing nothing for their place in society circles, so one day the King reluctantly called Matenko to his chambers and said, "Matenko, I'm sorry, but we're letting you go. I'm afraid you are too old and weak these days to be the jester we need. We have had a cottage built for you in your village and here's a bag of gold as a pension. Goodbye and many thanks for all your jesting."

Matenko was heartbroken. Though happy in performance, in private he was sorrowful, and now he was so down he almost sank right down into his pointed shoes with bells on the end. Soon, the gold pension ran out, and as Matenko was too old and weak to work on the farms he could make no money. His wife looked for work cleaning, but there was no one in the village who could pay to have their housework done. Matenko and his wife became very cold and hungry and they feared for their lives.

Then one day Matenko had an idea. "My dear, there is just one chance," sang Matenko to his wife. "Put on your best clothes, cut an onion up to create some tears, and go along to the palace to see the Queen…"

Matenko's wife did everything she was told. She put her best old frock on and went to see the Queen. "Poor old Matenko is dead," wept his wife. "He has worked so hard for you and now he lies dead in the tiny cold cottage you have given to us."

The Queen felt guilty and gave the woman 50 gold pieces for the funeral.

"Hurray!" shouted Matenko when his wife returned home with the money, and he danced an old reel around the cottage as he counted the money.

The next morning, it was Matenko's turn to go to the palace, but this time to see the King. With the help of a chopped onion, he wept to the King that his wife was dead and now he must live all on his own after such long service for his majesty.

Like the Queen, the King also felt guilty and gave Matenko a bag of gold.

"On the way out, Matenko," The king said, "ask cook to give you a cup of tea."

"Thank you so much, Your Majesty," Matenko said, still weeping.

After supping the tea, Matenko went skipping back to his wife with the gold.

"Blimey!" shouted Matenko when he looked in the moneybag. "200 gold pieces from the King. Woohoo!"

There was only one part of his master plan to go before Matenko could feel fully satisfied. On the sideboard of his house he lit two large funeral candles. He told his wife to lie down on the floor, cross her arms across her chest and pretend to be dead. Matenko did the same and he covered them both up with a large white shroud.

In the meantime, as soon as Metenko had left the palace, the King went to the Queen to tell her that the jester's wife was dead and how sad it was.

"It is not the jester's wife that is dead," replied the Queen. "It is the jester himself."

They began to quarrel about which of them was right until they both decided to visit the jester's house to see who was actually right.

When they knocked on the door, no one answered. The King slowly opened the door and peered inside. It was dark in the old cottage except for the two candles that burned lighting up the sheet where two bodies lay. It was clear that both were dead after all.

"But which of them died first?" asked the Queen. "It must have been Matenko."

"Oh don't talk daft," said the King. "It was his wife."

They began to quarrel again. Then suddenly Matenko jumped up from under the sheet with a big smile on his painted jester's face and said, "Your Majesty, my wife died first, but I was dead before her. Ha, ha, ha ha!"

"You old beggar!" laughed the King and Queen, rather pleased to find their dear old servants still alive. When Matenko and his wife tearfully explained how they nearly starved to death and had to hatch this tricky plan, the King and Queen felt ashamed. The royals promised to send the couple money whenever they needed it from then on.

The old jester and his wife lived well for the rest of their days, and Matenko would say, "You see, my dear, even an old jester can sometimes play a new trick."

The Weaving of a Dream

Once, in a land far to the east, there lived a widow and her three sons, Leme, Letuie and Leje. They lived a simple life: the young men chopped wood to sell and the old widow spent her days weaving brocades. She had a special gift for this and was well known for miles around for her beautiful brocades and tapestries. In her fingers they seemed to come alive with fruit and flowers, birds and animals.

One day, while she was at the market selling her work, she happened upon a stall displaying paintings. One of these, far more arresting than the others, caught her eye. It showed a palace overflowing with flowers and birds; fish swam in the river that ran through its gardens and a brilliant sun warmed its occupants with a glowing hue. Everything the old woman had ever dreamed about seemed encapsulated before her. Her heart was filled with joy as she examined every detail. Unable to stop herself, she traded all her brocades for the painting and returned home with this representation of her desires and dreams instead of rice for her sons. Three times she paused on her journey home to unroll the scroll and gaze at it in wonder. "If only I could live there," she whispered to herself.

At home Leme and Letuie were impatient with her. "What good is this to us?" they demanded crossly. "We cannot eat it."

Only her youngest son, Leje, understood his mother's dreams. "Mother," he suggested, "why don't you do a weaving of the painting? Your brocades are so lifelike it would almost be like living there."

"Yes, my son," she replied, "you are right. That is the nearest I will ever come to living there. I must do this or I will die of sorrow."

She set to work that very night, and once she started she simply didn't stop. As days passed into weeks, and weeks into months, the widow worked on and on.

Leme and Letuie chided their mother, telling her that they were tired of having to earn all the money, but Leje intervened. "Let mother be," he insisted, "or else she will die of grief. I will chop more wood."

So the old widow continued to weave, working all day and well into the night, when she had to work by candlelight. The smoke from the candles burned her eyes and made them red and sore.

After a year, when tears caused by the candlelight fell, she wove them into the fishpond and flowing river.

After two years, when her worn fingers spilt drops of blood upon the shuttle, she wove these into the glowing sun and scarlet flowers.

After three years she finished it.

It was the most beautiful brocade ever seen. The palace was woven in rich hues, its glorious gardens strewn with flowers. Tiny songbirds seemed to sing from the surface; fish swam; the river sparkled; and the red sun warmed every silken thread.

The widow rubbed her eyes, and a smile spread across her lined face. Her sons stood admiring her work, when suddenly a great wind blew open the door of their hut. It raced into the room, whipped the brocade from the loom and whisked it out of the open window and up into the sky.

The boys rushed outside, calling and shouting and chasing, but the brocade was gone. Returning to the hut, the sons found their mother fallen on the doorstep. She had collapsed with the shock.

When she came round, she pleaded with her eldest son to go east, to follow the wind and find her brocade. "It means more to me than my own life," she told him earnestly.

Leme set out straight away, and a month later came to the top of a mountain on which was perched a strange house made of stone. An old crone, sitting outside her home, enquired where he was heading.

"I'm going east," said Leme, "to where the wind has carried off a beautiful brocade my mother has spent three long years weaving."

"Ah, that," nodded the fortune teller knowingly. "The fairies of Sun Mountain sent the wind to bring it to them. They wish to copy its beautiful design. It certainly is a difficult and dangerous journey."

"How do I get there?" demanded Leme.

"First, you must knock out your two front teeth and place them in the mouth of my stone horse. He will then be able to eat the ten red berries growing on this bush. He will carry you to the fairies of Sun Mountain, but on the way you must pass over Flame Mountain. I warn you, you must not call out, even if the pain is unbearable, for if you do you will be burned to ashes. Next, you will come to the Sea of Ice – again, although it will be bitterly cold, you must not make a sound, or your body will be dashed to the bottom of the sea. If you pass through these places, you will reach Sun Mountain where you may be given your mother's brocade."

Leme shivered. He felt both hot and cold with fear. His face grew pale; he shook his head. The fortune teller cackled, "Young man, it seems you could not endure it, and after all you need not. Take this box of gold with you and go home to your mother."

Leme, pleased at this turn of events, hurried away from the fortune teller with the gold, and realising how much more he would have if he kept it to himself, took a different path at the foot of the mountain and headed towards the big city.

At home, Letuie and Leje waited with their mother, who was growing weaker by the day. When three months had passed and no word from Leme had come, the old woman asked Letuie to go east and find her brocade. "It means more to me than my own life," she told him.

So Letuie set out and soon found himself talking to the crone at the door of the stone house. He listened to her tale of fire and ice, and how he must knock out his two front teeth, and he shivered and shook his head. He was sent home with a box of gold, but being a greedy youth he too went to the big city to spend this fortune on himself.

The old widow waited, hoping daily for her sons' return with the precious brocade.

Finally, Leje could stand it no longer. He persuaded his mother that he would go east and find both the life-giving brocade and his brothers, who must surely be injured, trapped or unwell.

In half the time it had taken his brothers, Leje found his way to the fortune teller's house. She repeated the instructions and he stood firm before her, refusing her offer of gold. "I must fetch my mother's brocade or she will surely die," he told her.

Picking up a stone, he knocked out his two front teeth and placed them in the mouth of the stone horse. After the horse had eaten the ten berries, Leje jumped onto its back and clung on tightly as the amazing creature leapt high into the sky. It chased after the wind for three days and three nights until they reached Flame Mountain. The heat was unbearable. The stone horse plunged through the fire and Leje felt flames biting through his flesh, but he clenched his teeth, closed his eyes and did not cry out.

In half a day's time, they came out of the flames and stood on the shores of the Sea of Ice. Leje spurred his horse onwards and steam began to rise from his body as the ice-cold water stung his skin. He felt a bitter numbness descend, but uttered no sound at all. In half a day's time he came through the Sea of Ice, and there before him stood the fairies' palace on Sun Mountain. The warmth of the sun comforted him and began to ease the pain and heal his wounds.

Drifting from the open windows of the palace Leje could hear the sounds of women singing, talking and laughing. Down from his horse he jumped, and without fear opened the palace door and strode inside. He found himself in a great hall filled with fairies, all weaving as fast as they could to copy his mother's brocade which hung in the very centre of the room.

At the sight of this mortal the fairies froze, their eyes spreading panic. Leje quietly explained his mission and his mother's dreams and gradually the fairies' fear subsided. They asked him to stay with them for one night so he could regain his strength, as this would allow them a final night of weaving to finish their work. Leje agreed, ate the food prepared for him and fell into a deep and healing sleep.

The fairies did not sleep, however. When the sun set, a shining pearl was hung up to fill the room with light so that they could continue weaving. Later, the finest fairy weaver, on finishing her section, was disappointed when she found that compared to the widow's brocade hers was poor. "The original is so perfect, a real palace of paradise," thought the fairy, and so she began to weave herself into the old widow's brocade as a tiny red fairy dancing in a ray of sunshine.

At first light, the exhausted fairies finally slept, but Leje awoke, took down his mother's brocade and ran to his waiting horse. Three days and three nights later, he stood before the fortune teller's house. She congratulated him and, taking his teeth from the stone horse's mouth, she placed them back in Leje's mouth. It was as if they had never gone.

"Quickly, you must return home," she told him, "for your mother is dying of grief and is as weak as a single thread of silk. Wear these embroidered boots. They will speed you on your way."

In almost an instant, Leje was at his mother's side. He spread the brocade over her feeble form and the warmth of its sun began to draw her back into life. The old woman gazed happily at this weaving of her dream and noticed with surprise the tiny red fairy. Her thin fingers gently touched the woven fairy, and a gentle breeze danced in through the window.

It seemed that as the breeze blew, the brocade grew larger and taller, longer and wider until its silken threads covered everything in sight. The old hut disappeared and before their very eyes the brocade came to life. The palace, the gardens, the songbirds, the sun and even the red fairy all became real.

So it was that the widow's dream was woven into being through the love one son bore for his mother.

It is said that Leje married the red fairy and that Leme and Letuie returned when they heard people talk of their mother's fortunes. I believe that when they saw her happiness and thought of their desertion, they crept away shamefaced; they had taken no part in the weaving of her dream. I wonder… did you?

The Call of the Sea

If you go walking along Bonuit beach when the tide is out, you will see rock pools that hold limpets and sea urchins that the great tides forgot when they retreated.

It was like this the evening Joseph Rolande strolled on the beach after a long day's fishing. The sunset gave the water a rosy tinge and all was tranquil. Suddenly the peace was interrupted by the cry of a young woman: "Please! Help me, help me, brave sailor."

Joseph ran towards the voice and came upon a young woman up to her waist in seawater in a rock pool. She was crying into her long, salt-spangled hair.

"Help me please, I tarried too long and the tide has gone out and left me. Carry me back to the sea or I shall surely die."

As the woman said this, a large fin flipped the water and Joseph could see that the bottom half of this beautiful woman was as of a fish!

"No, oh no, no. You're a mermaid," said Joseph as he staggered back. "I know what mermaids do to men; they lure them down to the sea to drown."

"I will die if I dry, kind man," sobbed the mermaid.

Joseph was a kind man, so he lifted the lovely creature from the pool and carried her to the sea. He gently lowered her into the water. The mermaid swam around in the shallows, nuzzling Joseph's legs in pleasure and gratitude.

"Thank you," she cried. "If you come with me now, my father will reward you. He is King of the sea kingdom and has many treasures from the depths of the ocean."

"No, no, thank you," said Joseph as he stumbled back from the cold water. "Be off with you. I won't be lured to my death, never mind your father's treasures or your beauty."

"Then take this," said the mermaid, pushing an amber comb into Joseph's hand. "If you ever need me, pass it three times through the water and I shall come to you."

And with a thrash of her tail she disappeared under the foaming currents of the sea.

Joseph became obsessed with the wonderful creature. He tried to fight his thoughts, but every time he closed his eyes, all he could see was her face and her gleaming blue eyes. In the evenings, when the tide was out, he would walk along the shore in hope of catching sight of the swish of her golden tail or the shine of her long hair. Sometimes he would wade into the sea, searching the waves for a glimpse of his mermaid.

"So this is the magic you weave is it?" thought Joseph as he lay awake one night. "This is how you intend to lure me to my death. Well you won't win."

The next day, Joseph left his job as a fisherman, moved inland and bought a smallholding where he kept pigs. He had put a mountain between him and the sea. But the rain that spat on Joseph's tin roof was washed in from the coast. It was sea rain that kept him awake at night.

One night, a storm blew up that no one had seen the like of before. A ship was blown onto Bonuit rocks, and the Bonuit maroons were sounded.

All that could came out to peer through the rain that beat on their faces. Waves of great height fell upon the shoreline, overturning and smashing all that they touched. Beyond the sounds of the waves the heartbreaking cries of men and women clinging to the wreckage of the ship could be heard.

"It's hopeless. No one can get to them in this weather," said one Jerseyman.

"Help me launch the boat; it's not too late," shouted a determined voice behind them. Joseph Rolande came running down the beach. He had run all the way from his house behind the mountain, dressed in his fisherman's clothes.

The people watched with dread as his boat disappeared behind the mountains of waves that crashed around. Lightning lit up the scene and sent fear through all who stood helpless on dry land. Suddenly a gasp went up from an old fisherman watching from the bay. "Look!" he called. "Joseph – out there – and look, do you see the gigantic fish that follows him? No – it's a woman!"

"You called me with my comb, my friend and I have come to you," called the mermaid.

Her voice was as music to Joseph. "Help me save these people," he shouted to her.

And she did. With tender care, she lifted each one and carried them to Joseph's boat, planting them safely inside.

The sailors and passengers, deranged with fear, could hardly remember how it was they had escaped death. But later, many spoke of a woman's silky soft arms and tender care, and of a man both laughing and crying as he helped them on board.

As the boat carried the people to shore, the mermaid swam alongside. "I thought you had forgotten me, Joseph," she cried.

"I thought your kind were evil. I was wrong. Thank you for helping me," Joseph replied through his tears.

He helped the people onto the shore; then began to turn the boat around. Had he seen another soul to rescue?

"Don't go back; you've done enough. You will be taken by the wind and the tide," warned those on land.

But Joseph did put out to sea. And he never returned. Someone was waiting for him beyond the third wave, someone with the key to a kingdom way below the sea.

How the Sun Came Into the World

In the dreamtime, before men came into the world, there was no sun – only the distant moon – and the birds and animals had to creep about among the shadows and the darkness. The animals did not complain, for they knew of no alternative, but there were many accidents as the animals bumped into one another, trod on one another and peered warily into the inky blackness.

One day, on the edge of the Murrumbidgee River, the Emu and the Brolga fell to fierce fighting. As they screeched at each other in anger, their quarrel could be heard by all around as it echoed up the valley.

Brolga suddenly lunged forward and, seizing one of Emu's huge eggs, she hurled it with all her might up into the dark sky. Up and up it soared, up past the thick cloud layer, up into the infinite space beyond. There it fell upon a pile of firewood, burst its yolk and set light to the kindling. The fire blazed in the sky, and the animals below were amazed, their eyes dazzled by the light.

For the first time the animals could see each other clearly; they could view the world around them; they could move with confidence. They looked and looked. Some began to explore their new environment; others basked in the warmth thrown down. All too soon, however, the fire in the sky burned out and the Earth returned to darkness.

A kindly Sky Spirit had seen the animals' pleasure at the light and their dismay at the dark. He determined to light a new fire. All that night the Sky Spirit and his many helpers worked in the heavens gathering wood, and when the next day was due to begin the Spirit made ready to light the fire.

He sent the Morning Star to shine on the animals to warn them that the fire was about to be lit, so that they would not be afraid when the flames crackled and light dawned. But very few creatures noticed the Morning Star's gentle gleam; most of them remained in deep slumber.

So the Sky Spirit turned to Gougourhgah, the Kookaburra, and asked him if he would awaken the animals with his loud and braying call.

Gougourhgah was well pleased with this honour. He sat on a branch of an old gum tree and called, "Gou-gour-gah-ghah, gou-gour-gah-ghah, gou-gour-gah-ghah!"

Every creature on the plains beside the Murrumbidgee River awoke, and the great fire in the sky was kindled. Throughout the morning, the fire burned brighter and brighter, and as midday approached the flames grew hotter and hotter, sending bright light and intense heat to the Earth below.

Towards the close of day, the strength of the fire began to abate, and the red and golden rays of the very first sunset were seen. The wise Sky Spirit wrapped the dying embers of the fire in clouds to preserve them until the morning, when he used them to light another fire.

As far as I know, he has continued doing so from that day to this. As for the Kookaburra, he continues to call before each dawn, and when Man came to inhabit the Earth he learned to honour the great Kookaburra who welcomed the sun each morning. Children were forbidden to laugh at the Kookaburra's big mouth and strident call. "For if you insult Gougourhgah the Kookaburra," their parents told them, "he may take offence and not greet the Sun for us each day."

It is said that if the children defied their parents and poked fun at the Kookaburra, an extra tooth would grow near their eye-teeth and everyone would know they had laughed at Gougourhgah who brought the Sun into their world. "Gou-gour-gah-ghah, gou-gour-gah-ghah, gou-gour-gah-ghah!"

George and the Dragon

A Persian legend

The sun rose over the hill as the castle gates were cranked open from inside. A goose and a nanny goat wandered out. The gate clanked closed behind them with a great cloud of dust.

All that could be heard was the occasional honk of the goose and the sound of the bell that hung round the goat's neck.

Then, all at once, a seething, hissing noise could be discerned; then an immense shadow engulfed the two animals. In a sudden flash of flame and smoke the creatures were gone. The dragon had been fed for one more day.

The people who lived in the castle were prisoners in their fortified home. The whole population had been besieged by the dragon – a beast that stank of wilted flowers and rotting apples. A beast that had suddenly appeared from the great lake one day, hungry for flesh.

The sound of crying and wailing now came from every home within the castle. All the animals had been fed to the dragon. The king had ordered a lottery be drawn up with the name of every man, woman and child entered therein. Whosoever's name was drawn was turned out to be the dragon's food.

One day there came a knocking on the door of the king's chamber. A servant brought news that the name of the king's daughter, Princess Sabrina, had been drawn and that she was to be the next feast for the monster.

"No, no!" the king wailed. "Her name should never have been entered! My beloved daughter, my beautiful young, charming, clever daughter."

But other people had lost their loved ones and they demanded the king make the sacrifice too.

So, Princess Sabrina was tied to a flag post outside the gate in the same way as others before her had been. She squinted into the sun and her hair flitted across her eyes as she looked for the monster.

Suddenly, a horseman appeared over the hill, just as the beast rose from the lake. A hot blast of acrid air came from its direction. Sabrina screamed as the beast opened its drooling jaws. She closed her eyes and, just as the long green tongue began to wrap around her, a pained screech came from deep in the animal's body and its tongue slithered to the back of its mouth. The dragon turned and wailed as it looked down upon a silver spear thrust into its belly.

Fire gushed into the air as the beast raged against a knight who stood smiling up at his foe. "Come and get me, Egg Breath!" called the knight. He ran behind the monster, drawing his sword and smiting the end off the scaly tail.

The dragon turned wildly, flashing the remains of its tail, but just as it spun, the knight's sword was pushed with huge force right into the beast's heart. The creature crashed whimpering to the floor, exhaling for the last time in a bloody, smoky gurgle.

The knight turned to the princess, who looked on with bewilderment and great relief as he introduced himself. "Good job I turned up, eh? My name's George."

The castle gates were opened with a great cheer and the people poured out and danced around the cooling corpse of the dragon. The king embraced the knight and thanked him many times. "Stay, stay, my good man. Marry Sabrina and rule over the kingdom together after I'm dead," the king insisted.

George thanked him politely and exchanged smiles with the princess, but remounted his horse. "I'm sorry, Sire, but I am on a journey which does not end here."

And with that he rode away, watched by the whole town. As he began to disappear, they noticed that his shield was embellished with a cross, a simple blood-red cross.

The Old Woman in the Wood

A Grimms tale retold

One day, a young servant girl was travelling through some dark, dense forest-land with the family she was in service with, when suddenly they were attacked by robbers. The brutal brigands killed all they could find – man, woman and child. The young girl was the only one to survive, as she had been able to hide herself behind a bush just off the road. When the robbers had gone, she came out to face the ugly sight of the carnage they had left. The only sound was the song of birds in the trees that flitted innocently above the young servant-girl's head. The peace was in marked contrast to the sounds of killing and destruction there had been a moment before. The girl sat down upon a stone and cried bitterly. "What is a poor girl like me to do, cold, defenceless and lost in this deep dark forest? I will certainly starve to death or be eaten by wild animals."

Suddenly, from out of the trees, came a white dove. It had a little golden key in its beak. It dropped the key in the girl's soft hand, saying, "Do you see that tree over there, the large one covered with soft green moss? Find the small keyhole and you will find food and drink."

Half in disbelief, the girl rose and ran to the tree. She did as the dove had told her, and sure enough there was a plate of ginger biscuits and cold milk within the trunk – plenty to satisfy her hungry tummy.

When she had eaten her fill, she called to the dove, saying, "It is surely the time when at home the hens will be going to roost. I am so tired, but I have no straw to sleep under tonight."

Again, the dove flew to her and placed another tiny golden key in the girl's hand. "Open that tree over there and you will find a bed," said the dove.

The girl found the tree, and feeling round its mossy rough bark with her fingers, she found the keyhole. She fitted the key in the lock and turned. There inside was a beautiful bed, laid with fine white silken sheets.

The girl fell on the bed and sank into a deep sleep, the like of which she had never had before.

In the morning, when the young girl had woken from her dreams, the dove came for a third time. "Open the large tree that stands over there and you will find some fine fresh clothes to wear."

When the girl opened this tree there were splendid clothes beset with gold and

jewels, more
splendid than a king's
daughter would ever wear.

So, the girl lived like this for some time
– a princess of the woods, her every wish fulfilled by the doting dove.

One day the dove said, "Will you do something for me?"

"With all my heart," replied the girl.

The dove said, "I will guide you through the forest to a small house. Enter it.
Inside, an old woman will be sitting by a fire and she will say, "Good day", but on
your life you must give no answer to her. Let her do what she will, but make sure you
pass by her on her right side. Further on there is a door; open it and you will enter
a room where there is a quantity of rings upon a large oak table. There will be very
beautiful ones sparkling with stones, but leave them and look for the plain one, which
will be among the others, and bring it here to me as fast as you can."

The dove took the girl to the little house that sat on its own in the wood. Smoke
rose from the chimney, and a few hens pecked around at the grass that lay about
the house. The young girl went through the door. There sat the old woman who
stared when she saw the girl, and said, "Good day, my child." The girl, terrified but
determined to carry out the dove's instructions, gave no answer, walked past and
opened the door.

"Wither away!" cried the old woman and seized the girl's gown, trying to hold her
fast with her gnarled old hands. "This is my house. No one can go in there if I choose
not to allow it."

But the girl ignored her and headed straight into the room, pushing the old woman
away from her on to the floor.

On the table lay an enormous quantity of shiny rings, which gleamed and glittered in front of the anxious eyes of the girl. She shuffled through them and turned them all over, desperately looking for a plain one, but she could not find it.

While she was looking she heard a dull knock from behind her and as she turned she saw the old woman attempting to steal out of the room, grasping an old birdcage as she went. The girl stopped what she was doing and bravely marched over to the old woman. Looking her straight in the face she pulled the cage from out of the old woman's cold grasp. The girl raised it up and looked inside. Sure enough, there, in the bill of the frightened bird in the cage, was the plain gold ring she wanted so dearly. She opened the cage and took the ring. Dropping the cage and releasing the bird, she ran back joyously to meet the dove that she was sure would be waiting for her.

When the relieved young girl arrived at the place where she had been living, no dove was there to greet her. She leant against a tree to wait for her dove. As she stood thus, she stroked the soft moss that grew on the tree behind her as she had often done, but this time the tree seemed to have become soft and pliant, warm and tender. The branches began to twine around her, and suddenly she realised that they were not branches at all, but the arms of a man. Turning round swiftly, she realised she was in the warm embrace of a handsome young man, who kissed her gently.

"You have delivered me from the curse of the old woman, who is really a witch." he explained. "She had changed me into a tree and for two hours every day I was a white dove. As long as she possessed the ring I would never be able to resume my human shape and existence."

Looking around her, the girl then saw other trees turning back into the young man's servants and horses, who had likewise been transformed and were now freed from the enchantment like their master. They headed to the young man's kingdom— for he was a prince. He married the girl and together they lived happily ever after.